NEW DIRECTIONS FOR EVALUATION
A Publication of the American Evaluation Association

Lois-ellin G. Datta, *Datta Analysis*
EDITOR-IN-CHIEF

Advances in Survey Research

Marc T. Braverman
University of California, Davis

Jana Kay Slater
California Department of Education

EDITORS

Number 70, Summer 1996

JOSSEY-BASS PUBLISHERS
San Francisco

ADVANCES IN SURVEY RESEARCH
Marc T. Braverman, Jana Kay Slater (eds.)
New Directions for Evaluation, no. 70
Lois-ellin G. Datta, Editor-in-Chief

Microfilm copies of issues and articles are available in 16mm and 35mm, as well as microfiche in 105mm, through University Microfilms Inc., 300 North Zeeb Road, Ann Arbor, Michigan 48106-1346.

ISSN 0164-7989   ISBN 0-7879-9904-0

NEW DIRECTIONS FOR EVALUATION is part of The Jossey-Bass Education Series and is published quarterly by Jossey-Bass Inc., Publishers, 350 Sansome Street, San Francisco, California 94104-1342.

Subscriptions for 1996 cost $59.00 for individuals and $87.00 for institutions, agencies, and libraries.

EDITORIAL CORRESPONDENCE should be addressed to the Editor-in-Chief, Lois-ellin G. Datta, P.O. Box 383768, Waikoloa, HI 96738.

EDITORIAL POLICY AND PROCEDURES

NEW DIRECTIONS FOR EVALUATION, a quarterly sourcebook, is an official publication of the American Evaluation Association. The journal publishes empirical, methodological, and theoretical works on all aspects of evaluation and related fields. Substantive areas may include any program, field, or issue with which evaluation is concerned, such as government performance, tax policy, energy, environment, mental health, education, job training, medicine, and public health. Also included are such topics as product evaluation, personnel evaluation, policy analysis, and technology assessment. In all cases, the focus on evaluation is more important than the substantive topics. We are particularly interested in encouraging a diversity of evaluation perspectives and experiences and in expanding the boundaries of our field beyond the evaluation of social programs.

The editors do not consider or publish unsolicited single manuscripts. Each issue of the journal is devoted to a single topic, with contributions solicited, organized, reviewed, and edited by a guest editor. Issues may take any of several forms, such as a series of related chapters, a debate, or a long article followed by brief critical commentaries. In all cases, the proposals must follow a specific format, which can be obtained from the editor-in-chief. These proposals are sent to members of the editorial board and to relevant substantive experts for peer review. The process may result in acceptance, a recommendation to revise and resubmit, or rejection. However, the editors are committed to working constructively with potential guest editors to help them develop acceptable proposals.

Lois-ellin G. Datta, Editor-in-Chief
P.O. Box 383768
Waikoloa, HI 96738

Jennifer C. Greene, Associate Editor
Department of Human Service Studies
Cornell University
Ithaca, NY 14853-4401

Gary Henry, Associate Editor
Public Administration and Urban Studies
Georgia State University
Atlanta, GA 30302-4039

CONTENTS

7. Translating Survey Questionnaires: Lessons Learned   93

Ruth B. McKay, Martha J. Breslow, Roberta L. Sangster,
Susan M. Gabbard, Robert W. Reynolds, Jorge M. Nakamoto, John Tarnai

Three case studies illustrate the theoretical and logistical issues associated with different translation approaches.

EDITORS' NOTES

We would hazard a guess that it is the rare evaluator who has never designed and implemented a survey as a form of data collection. Clearly, surveys are a fundamental mode of research across all the social sciences. Therefore, we are pleased to be offering a volume of *New Directions for Evaluation* that focuses on recent lines of theory and research related to survey methods. This is the first issue of the journal to be devoted to surveys in twelve years. Both survey research and evaluation research have grown considerably in those years, so we feel the topic is particularly timely.

One question we considered when assembling the volume is whether there are survey issues uniquely relevant for evaluation. That is, do evaluators need certain kinds of information that are absent from the larger survey literature? We determined that there may indeed be some special relevance for evaluators in questions about how surveys are used, but in general, the considerations relating to good survey research apply also to good use of surveys in evaluation. These articles reflect that view.

In Chapter One, Gary Henry challenges our field to enhance the democratic nature of evaluation practice by using surveys to involve the public in policy discourse. In Chapter Two, Marc Braverman provides an overview of recent survey research through an analysis of the components of survey error.

Chapters Three through Five focus on methodological elements of survey design and implementation. In Chapter Three, Jon Krosnick and his colleagues present a theory of the factors determining whether a respondent will invest the cognitive effort necessary to provide high-quality answers to survey questions. Don Dillman and his colleagues, in Chapter Four, review types of effects that have been attributed to the mode of survey administration, particularly telephone and mail. Mick Couper and Robert Groves, in Chapter Five, describe theoretical perspectives on survey nonresponse, examining whether these perspectives are supported by data from the U.S. Census and several other large-scale national surveys.

Chapter Six addresses the phase of survey data analysis. Kathy Green proposes use of the Rasch model to examine survey data and make postsurvey adjustments to improve the validity of measures. Finally, in Chapter Seven, Ruth McKay and her colleagues address a special topic that is growing ever more critical for survey practitioners: the need to produce surveys in languages other than English to reach non-English-speaking populations.

We would like to acknowledge and thank our New Directions associate editor, Gary Henry, as well as our colleagues who served as reviewers for earlier drafts of these chapters: Curt Acredolo, Alan Fenech, and Xiaojia Ge of the University of California, Davis; Joel Moskowitz of the University of California,

Berkeley; Judy Boser of the University of Tennessee; Chet McCall of Pepperdine University; and Sharon McNeely of Northeastern Illinois University.

In this brief volume, we felt the weight of space limitations strongly. There are many topics we wish we had the opportunity to present, such as recent advances in technological aspects of data collection and new data analysis procedures appropriate for survey contexts. However, we must leave those topics for a future team of ambitious editors. In the meantime, we are pleased to have played a role in developing a volume that offers a rich diversity of perspectives on the changing field of survey research.

Marc T. Braverman
Jana Kay Slater
Editors

MARC T. BRAVERMAN *is a Cooperative Extension specialist in the Department of Human and Community Development and director of the 4-H Center for Youth Development at the University of California, Davis.*

JANA KAY SLATER *is a research and evaluation consultant with the California Department of Education.*

Surveys can be a powerful tool for engaging the public in evaluation.

Does the Public Have a Role in Evaluation? Surveys and Democratic Discourse

Gary T. Henry

Surveys are prominent icons in both evaluation research and the American political landscape. As measures of the political and social culture, polls—as surveys are so often called in the popular press—report on what we think and feel and do. Political and social surveys cut across lines of race, class, and social status that most of us seldom cross in daily life. They give us a broader sense of public opinion than we can develop from our own experience. Most often, we see in the media the results of general population surveys, which are surveys of a sample of adults in the nation, a region, a state, or a community. We embrace these results as sources of information, yardsticks against which to measure our own opinions and behaviors, and guides for action. Survey results are considered so potent in the world's democratic political cultures that, in several countries, surveys are banned or their results embargoed immediately before elections. Evaluation research has not yet fully capitalized on either the potential or the potency of surveys.

Evaluators use surveys extensively. This volume substantiates the interest among evaluators in survey research and the importance of surveys for

The author expresses thanks to Jana Kay Slater and Marc Braverman for their deft editorial work on earlier drafts. Much of the research reported in this chapter was supported by the Applied Research Center and Georgia State University.

evaluation. However, evaluators have typically viewed surveys from a means-ends perspective, seeing surveys as instruments or technical devices. Advances in the methodology of data collection have enhanced the quality and accuracy of data used in evaluations. But progress has been slower in exploring and extending the uses of surveys in evaluation and the ways in which results might be communicated to a broad range of audiences.

Evaluators most often survey a sample of one or more groups of stakeholders to gather information on stakeholder behaviors and opinions that relate to the evaluation questions at hand. For example, evaluations of welfare reform might survey welfare recipients to determine their employment status, wage rates, hours of employment, education and training activities, means of transportation to work, family composition, child care arrangements, and services actually received as a part of the reform. Evaluators may also inquire about attitudes that relate to finding a job or opinions about quality of life and participation in the welfare program. These examples point to the nature of the groups surveyed in most evaluations—special populations. Only in the area of needs assessments are broader populations frequently surveyed, and even then, it is often to determine their eligibility for or interest in being included in a special population.

In general, evaluators seek little information from the general public, information that could be useful in framing evaluation questions or in obtaining reactions to evaluation recommendations. This is remarkable in this day when few public policies are changed without the benefit of a poll. If evaluations indeed find their uniqueness in their use of systematically collected data to inform public policy or program decisions (Rossi and Freeman, 1993), the omission of data from the public regarding evaluation design and recommendations is striking. In fact, it is plausible that a lack of this type of information in political environments that are otherwise replete with it from other, often biased sources (Greider, 1992) has reduced the utilization of evaluation findings.

Furthermore, the information from evaluations is often not shared with the public in a way that may inform their opinions about social conditions or proposed changes in a policy. The evaluation community has long regarded stakeholders and decision makers as key audiences for evaluation findings. We have, however, taken such a limited view of the audience that the concept of democratic evaluation only applies to those whose livelihoods are directly affected by a program (MacDonald, 1976; Shadish, Cook, and Leviton, 1991). Thus, for example, in the case of educational evaluation, it appears that MacDonald's criterion for democratic evaluation would be met simply by including teachers in the evaluation process.

Certainly, significant stakeholders such as teachers must be included under the umbrella of democratic evaluation in education; however, their inclusion seems insufficient to meet a criterion of democratic inclusion. Members of the general public also have a large stake in such areas as education and, through elected representatives, a strong influence over the utilization of evaluation results. For example, however we as individuals feel about the current direction of welfare reform, we cannot mistake the fact that the public register serious concerns about the abuse of the current system and support the direction of the reforms, thus lending strength to the process. It is ironic that even evaluations conceived to be democratic exclude a role for citizens.

This chapter considers three ways in which surveys can be, but usually are not, used in evaluation:

To frame the evaluation question. General population surveys can be used to gauge opinions and information about a policy or program, for use in framing evaluation questions.

To provide context for evaluation recommendations. General population surveys can be used to measure opinions about evaluation conclusions in order to provide policy makers with an expanded context for making decisions.

To communicate evaluative information to the public. Survey data and other evaluation findings can be used to inform the public.

Each of these uses goes beyond the current and extremely important use of surveys of special populations to gather information about the need for, or effects and implementation of, a policy. Each application stretches the notion of evaluation and has a potential impact on the use of evaluation and the integration into evaluation of the Jeffersonian ideal of an informed citizenry as the best defense of democracy.

In the next three sections, each of these suggestions for using surveys in evaluations is explored. The first two sections focus on ways in which general population surveys may identify target areas for evaluation research and assist decision makers. At the beginning of an evaluation and at its conclusion, surveys can powerfully enhance the potential uses of evaluation results. The third section discusses how survey information can attract media and public attention to evaluation findings.

Who Knows? Who Cares? Framing
Evaluation Questions

Evaluators have a strong implicit belief that good decisions are based on good information. Indeed, evaluators provide much of the good information that is available for decision making. When public policies and programs are to be evaluated, the information on which members of the public base their opinions can be a vital link in the process of identifying important evaluation questions. Using surveys to understand public knowledge and sentiment about a public program fits the textbook definition of evaluation research (Rossi and Freeman, 1993, p. 5). However, public knowledge of social conditions and policy is limited and extremely varied. Some surveys, of the name-your-congressman type, for example, have shown low levels of civic knowledge (Carpini and Keeter, 1991) and low levels of knowledge about specific policies (for example, Kull, 1994).

Figure 1.1 shows the percentage of correct responses registered for twenty policy-related questions in a survey of the U.S. public in June 1993. On the eve of President Clinton's 1994 effort to reform the health care system, only 21 percent of the public knew that approximately 25 percent of Americans were uninsured. Inadequately informed, the public never developed a consensus about the extent or root of the problem. Consequently, public opinion never crystallized around any of the reform packages. Whether one supported reform or the status quo, it was clear in the debate that there were too little information, too many issues, and no consensus arising out of the lobbying and marketing campaigns. The public were being urged to express their opinions on a very important public policy issue without having much factual data. If good information leads to good decisions, we were unlikely at that time to have good decisions on health care reform. Crime and corrections, homelessness and mental illness, education and Head Start, and defense were the policy areas where the information base was most accurate. But as the country faced the most pressing issues of the day—decisions on health care, welfare policy, and the deficit—the public had inaccurate information about the social conditions related to these issues and the size of the problems.

Less than half of the respondents in the June 1993 poll knew that more children than seniors live in poverty. Of course, welfare reform, a major policy item on state and national policy agendas at the time of the survey, directly affects many of these children. It does not take a substantial leap to reach the implication that few had considered the impact of various welfare reform packages on children living in poverty. While Social Security, which has had a major impact on reducing poverty among senior citizens, was being kept off the table, welfare reform threatened to further impoverish many children's lives.

Welfare reform evaluations that influenced the original reforms of the late 1980s reported on the impact of reform on work and welfare costs (Szanton, 1991, p. 596); the impact on children's lives was omitted. The evaluations that were influential had two important characteristics. First, they measured the effects that were consistent with the way the issues were defined on the policy agenda and in the minds of the public (Kull, 1994). That is, the evaluations were framed to address critical issues—how to encourage welfare recipients to go to work and how to lower program costs. Second, according to Szanton, the experimental designs were considered definitive by the users of the research. This perception was a major factor in the designs' acceptance.

Both public misinformation and lack of information have direct implications for evaluation. The policies and programs that we spend much time evaluating are developed and changed in response to the way in which the problems they address are socially defined or constructed. "A condition that is defined as problematic thereby becomes a problem. Conversely, no social condition, no matter how irksome, is a social problem until it is defined as such

Figure 1.1. Public Information on Social Conditions and Policy Issues

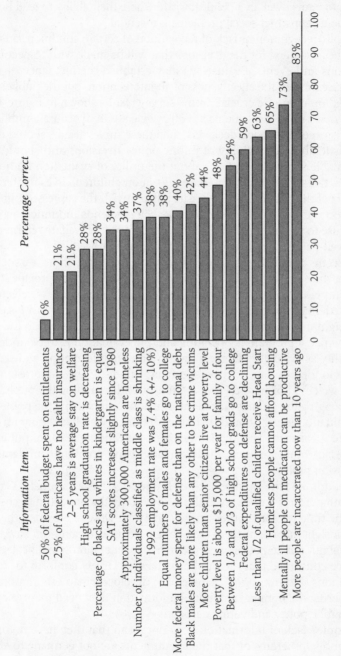

Information Item

Percentage Correct

- 50% of federal budget spent on entitlements — 6%
- 25% of Americans have no health insurance — 21%
- 2–5 years is average stay on welfare — 21%
- High school graduation rate is decreasing — 28%
- Percentage of blacks and whites in kindergarten is equal — 28%
- SAT scores increased slightly since 1980 — 34%
- Approximately 300,000 Americans are homeless — 34%
- Number of individuals classified as middle class is shrinking — 37%
- 1992 employment rate was 7.4% (+/- 10%) — 38%
- Equal numbers of males and females go to college — 38%
- More federal money spent for defense than on the national debt — 40%
- Black males are more likely than any other to be crime victims — 42%
- More children than senior citizens live at poverty level — 44%
- Poverty level is about $15,000 per year for family of four — 48%
- Between 1/3 and 2/3 of high school grads go to college — 54%
- Federal expenditures on defense are declining — 59%
- Less than 1/2 of qualified children receive Head Start — 63%
- Homeless people cannot afford housing — 65%
- Mentally ill people on medication can be productive — 73%
- More people are incarcerated now than 10 years ago — 83%

Source: Survey of a nationwide sample of U.S. residents conducted by the Georgia State University Applied Research Center, June 1993. A total of 933 respondents were randomly selected and surveyed by telephone.

in the arena of politics" (Rossi and Freeman, 1993, p. 61). Decision makers for public programs dwell in a political world where their ability to read how their constituents construct social problems is essential.

Public recognition or lack of recognition of certain conditions and events establishes a context for the decisions that will be made with respect to those conditions and events. Evaluations may establish the incidence or rates of occurrence or even the effectiveness of an intervention, but the public's assessment and opinions are crucial. In the survey results shown in Figure 1.1., we can see that public assessments are often inaccurate. If accurate public information is needed for good decisions, then these survey results should make us pessimistic about the quality of public policy decisions and should render questionable some assumptions about the utility of evaluation findings. For example, does the impact of welfare reform on children's lives matter if most members of the public define the issue differently? If the expressed public consensus on the welfare problem is that "society spends too much on women who refuse to work," then evaluations of the impact of welfare reform on children's well-being may have little chance of being utilized.

It seems reasonable to argue that evaluations must address issues in the way that they are defined by the public if evaluations are to provide information compelling to policy makers. After all, policy makers, elected and appointed, make program decisions within a political world. Surveys can provide insight into the public perception of a problem and establish the context within which a program is operating and the evaluation is to be undertaken. Our ability as evaluators to guess levels of public information and sentiment can be clouded by our own perspectives, interests, and circumstances. Of course, we could dismiss the importance of understanding the public's views by disparaging the public's lack of information, rationalizing the point of view that evaluation issues should be framed by those who have program knowledge and greater information. However, understanding levels of public information, lack of information, misinformation, and opinion is fundamental to the decision process.

In addition, the public's lack of knowledge has a rationale. Gathering information exacts a price, even if it is often only the opportunity cost of not using the time for some other activity. In 1957, Downs provided the fundamental insight that members of the public have little to gain from having information about public policies and programs. A generation of political scientists has since confirmed that the public's behaviors largely conform to "rational" expectations (Fiorina, 1990). People have developed many shortcut methods for gathering the minimal amount of information they need to form opinions about public policy and voting decisions.

People's lack of information does not mean that they have no opinions about public programs or that their sentiments are not germane to efforts to make changes based on evaluation results. General population surveys can provide a check on our assumptions about the social construction of problems. Surveys can provide insights about the issues that are of greatest interest to the public and can also expose myths that need to be confronted before other information can be used. If, as the survey presented earlier found, most people overestimate the amount of time the average welfare recipient spends on welfare, that misconception will need to be addressed in the evaluation before other information can be meaningfully considered.

I certainly do not advocate using public opinion surveys as the only method for identifying the questions to be addressed through an evaluation. Using welfare reform as an example again, the issues most salient to the public might be employment, reducing the number of children born to women on welfare, and program cost. Yet evaluation may also need to address the well-being and educational progress of children of families in poverty to provide a comprehensive assessment of the impacts of reform.

Evaluation may gain relevancy and increase utilization of its results by providing information on matters of public interest. Aligning evaluation measures to address issues salient to the public may not only increase public interest in findings but also provide information on issues central to the decision of policy makers—who will ultimately choose whether to use the evaluation findings when making their decisions.

Flag Waving in Peoria: Informing Policy Makers About Public Sentiment

Public sentiment often carries more weight in determining the fate of public programs than evaluation findings. Former President Nixon is said to have told advisers who came to him with proposals of one sort or another to run them up the flagpole in Peoria and see who salutes (Barone and Ujifusa, 1984, p. 367). (We cannot be sure, of course, whether Peoria represented middle America to the president or whether the reference was a nod to the power of Illinois Senator Dirksen when Nixon was vice president and presiding over the Senate.) "Running it up the flagpole" has endured in the political lexicon of our age. "Spin doctors" and candidates alike cite polls to lay claim to the imperative of public opinion in support of their positions.

Through general population surveys, we see who salutes. For example, the governor of Georgia recently commissioned a task force on schools and violence. Several polls had already established that the public viewed school violence as a major social problem and as their primary concern about public education (Johnson and Immerwahr, 1994). After receiving testimony and reviewing findings from experts and evaluators, the task force recommended nine actions, ranging from providing metal detectors in the schools to making parents legally responsible for actions of their children. The task force then commissioned a poll to determine the level of public support for each recommendation. Eight recommendations received approval ratings of about 75 percent or more. However, only 40 percent of Georgians approved of banning corporal punishment in the schools. As a result, the task force decided that abolishing corporal punishment should be removed from its legislative agenda, to avoid stalling the package over one issue. The eight remaining recommendations went to the legislature, and each was enacted. As this example illustrates, public opinion surveys can provide important information for crafting recommendations, setting the policy agenda, and influencing the adoption of program changes.

Polls also enable us to find out more than just broad brushstrokes of public opinion. Often policy makers want to know the reactions of specific groups. For example, elected officials want to know about voters from their districts or about specific groups of citizens likely to be interested in a particular issue.

As described in the previous section, misinformed or uninformed opinion is often the basis for the published poll results we see in print. A poll conducted by the Center for the Study of Policy Attitudes illustrates this problem. The public express very negative opinions about government welfare programs. However, their opinions are based on inaccurate information—in this poll, administrative costs were overestimated at 53 percent of total expenditures while they are actually about 12 percent; benefits to the poor were underestimated at about 11 percent of total expenditures while they actually represent at least 78 percent of expenditures (Kull, 1994). Understanding such gaps in information may influence the way in which evaluation data are used and interpreted.

Survey results such as these find a home in the increasingly sophisticated and often pseudoscientific environment of interest group politics (Greider, 1992). In this environment, evaluation results are touted by one group or another to the extent that they support the group's interests. Certainly, the "good government" and "better results" rationales borne under the evaluation mantle carry weight with legislators and program administrators. However, the commitment to using evaluation results is not independent of the course of action suggested by those results. Decisions are driven by what is possible, not necessarily by what is "best" by an evaluative criterion. This is political rationality. Long ago, Downs (1957, p. 35) proclaimed a fundamental concept of representative democracy: "The main goal of every party is the winning of elections. Thus, its actions are aimed at maximizing votes, and it treats policies merely as means towards this end." Policies are, in large measure, tools for getting reelected. Downs goes further to suggest that carried to the extreme, political rationality would mean that every elected official would determine the preferences of relevant voters and vote every issue according to a position that reflects these preferences. Savvy appointed administrators, in turn, would not press recommendations that would cause problems at the polls for elected officials, because then the administrators' own positions would be threatened in this entirely self-interested worldview.

Obviously, public opinion does not always dictate a politician's course of action to this extreme. In some cases, elected officials will be more interested in attempting to sway public opinion than simply following it. In 1992, reflecting the spirit of the New South, Governor Zell Miller of Georgia led such an effort, directed at removing the Confederate battle emblem from the Georgia state flag in spite of the fact that overall support for that change never climbed above 35 percent (see Figure 1.2), and only a bare majority of African Americans supported removing the emblem that many associate with racism. Lacking compelling strength from moral suasion, Governor Miller lost his fight in the legislature and recoiled from leadership on the issue. Evaluators must understand that elected officials do not blindly follow polls, but they do like to know what public opinion is on an issue. In some cases, politicians will attempt to do what they think is right and try either to turn public opinion in the desired direction or to place the decision making in an arena where public opinion is less influential, such as a nonelected board or commission. But polling results do allow elected officials to assess political feasibility and develop a viable strategy for implementing an evaluator's proposal or recommendation.

As in all things political, uncertainty and compromise figure into the forging of policy positions and the use of evaluation results. Checking out who salutes does not mean capitulating on evaluation recommendations. However, making recommendations often requires a leap from the data on impact and implementation (Hendricks, 1994). Findings are seldom clear enough or sufficiently generalizable to yield exact recommendations. A telephone survey of the general public concerning the recommendations arising from an evaluation could take ten minutes or less per interview and exact few costs from respondents, yet could establish public perceptions of problems and sentiments toward different recommendations and, in doing so, could add a democratic element to the evaluation. A recommendation that recognizes public sentiment or that describes the issue in the same terms used by the public may be more influential than other possible recommendations and may cause policy makers to recognize the relevance of evaluation in policy debates.

Who Will Tell the People? Informing the Electorate

In his 1992 book, *Who Will Tell the People,* William Greider gave a bleak perspective on the future of public policy making in the United States. Well-funded lobbyists who generate information and political demonstrations *du jour* to suit the interests of their clients are becoming the conduits of public opinion within capitols across the country. This scenario is not the wish of most Americans, however. Americans want to stay informed about public policy issues, with 82 percent reporting on the 1993 national survey cited above that they saw this as their duty; the same survey, however, showed that they do not translate duty into information. Cost trade-offs of time and resources were the limiting factors. As described earlier, Americans form opinions based on very little information and/or misinformation.

Who will provide information to the public? Do evaluation findings have a role in public discourse? What role is there for evaluators? Data on the state of policy knowledge, such as those presented in Figure 1.1, indicate that we are on thin ice if an informed electorate is the solidifying base of support for a

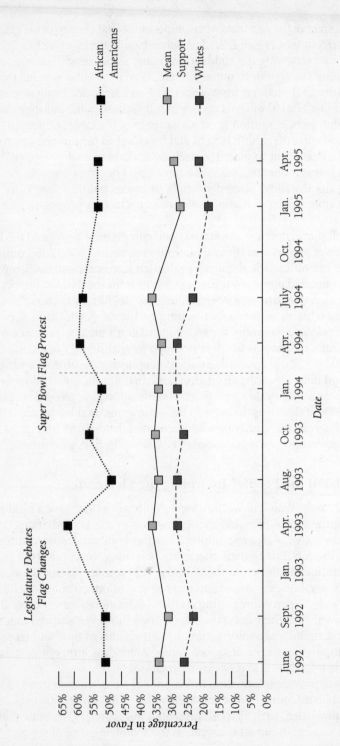

Figure 1.2. Support for Changing the Georgia State Flag

Source: Georgia State Polls of at least 800 Georgians, conducted by the Georgia State University Applied Research Center.

democracy. Information on program needs and program effects, intended and unintended, is the product of evaluations. The fact that evaluators are in the business of collecting this information brings this discussion of the relationship between evaluation and the public full circle. I began by exploring the public's degree of misinformation and the view that it is rational for members of the public to invest little in the acquisition of policy information. Rather than condemn their apparent apathy, I suggested that we recognize that their perceptions and sentiments often play a significant role in the political process including whether or not evaluation results are used. Now, we must consider the fact that evaluators not only can learn and sharpen their interactions in the policy process with information about public sentiment but also hold much of the information that could improve the accuracy of public policy knowledge. Yet there is little effort aimed at creating public discourse based on evaluation findings.

For many reasons, we should be skittish about entering into public discourse. First, when do we know enough to advocate a position? As scientists, we generally recognize the limitations of our findings. The tenets of science, as we perceive them, do not support broadcasting the findings of individual studies. Second, evaluators have a justified trepidation of upsetting sponsors by releasing evaluation findings that may not fully support sponsor preferences. This issue is being actively discussed in the evaluation community as we consider the ethical and practical conflicts between loyalties to clients and loyalties to providing neutral and uncompromised information. Certainly, surprising sponsors with information releases is not an appropriate method of operating. But under what circumstances, if any, should an evaluator inform the public about information that the sponsor would prefer to disregard?

A third concern for evaluators is the appearance of advocacy associated with releasing information and analysis. Once the barrier to the public is breached, evaluators become interested parties who appear to be favoring some positions and opposing others. Generally, the evaluator will be perceived as an advocate when recommendations are used in policy discussion, especially when the recommendations are considered controversial. When evaluators are perceived as advocates, will they, and perhaps their livelihoods, be compromised in the future?

After considering these issues, I believe that a strong case can be made for using evaluation results to inform the public. First, the research that is conducted is often the most rigorous and salient that is available. Second, I come back to the underlying belief that evaluation is a worthwhile activity: better information will lead to better decisions. Public opinion and the information on which public opinion is based often establish the political feasibility of any action recommended in an evaluation. Overly simplistic assumptions about a public program, uninformed by empirical data, can lead to overly simplistic solutions to social problems. Evaluation results have an important role in informing the citizenry. However, a pragmatic concern remains: how do we communicate the information to the public?

Citizens, rationally, will not allocate much time to obtaining evaluation information for themselves. Information that is to reach them must be easily accessible and readily retrievable. In other words, the message must get into the media. Once again, surveys have a role. Surveys create news. Consider for a moment the number of polls that are reported in the newspapers on any given day and the partnerships between news organizations and polling organizations. General population surveys provide a bridge between evaluation research and journalists who must find a way to make news out of research findings. By drawing out the conflicts between, on one hand, the public perception about a program or its clients and, on the other hand, the empirical results of the evaluation or the policy goals that would be supported by evaluation recommendations, evaluators can stimulate interest in the study results.

Informing the public completes the loop of connecting general public surveys in new and different ways to the field of evaluation. If an informed electorate is important for a democracy, improving the accuracy of information retained by the public is vital. The evaluator's role is central, and surveys can enhance evaluators' access to the media. This does not mean that the work will be easy. New skills and more funding are needed to add general population surveys to the lists of evaluation activities. But the evaluation community must answer the question, "If not evaluators, who?"

Conclusion

General population surveys have been used sparingly by evaluators, even though surveys of the public are a well-established and low-cost means of securing information on public sentiments about policy issues. Polls reveal that the public can recall little accurate information about social conditions or public policy. However, this does not constrain public opinion or limit its use in policy debates. Public opinion is central to any determination of the relevance and political feasibility of evaluation findings. Understanding public perceptions may help us frame evaluation questions that resonate with the public and policy makers alike. This may require adding more questions and collecting more data in an evaluation, but it may also create conditions that enhance the use of the findings. Avoiding language traps and politically loaded labels, while still communicating accurately, can be important in making recommendations in a political environment. For example, changing the term "welfare" to "assistance to the poor" greatly affects public reaction (Smith, 1987).

Finally, general population surveys are mirrors of the social landscape, reflecting a society's attitudes and behaviors. As individuals, we spend much time peering into that mirror. We compare ourselves to the norms that surveys create, and these norms often influence our own attitudes and behaviors. Newspapers and other news media have picked up on our interest in survey results and feed them to us in a seemingly endless supply. Evaluators can capitalize on the interest in survey results of both the media and the public. Surveys can pique journalists' interest in evaluation results. They can expose myths or misconceptions about a program or its clients. Surveys can be an important means of motivating media attention to evaluation findings and, in turn, enhancing the public's knowledge about the operation and effectiveness of public programs.

References

Barone, M., and Ujifusa, G. *The Almanac of American Politics*. Washington, D.C.: The National Journal, 1984.

Carpini, M.X.D., and Keeter, S. "Stability and Change in the U.S. Public's Knowledge of Politics." *Public Opinion Quarterly*, 1991, *55*, 583–612.

Downs, A. *An Economic Theory of Democracy*. New York: HarperCollins, 1957.

Fiorina, M. "Information and Rationality in Elections." In J. A. Ferejohn and J. H. Kuklinski (eds.), *Information and Democratic Processes*. Urbana: University of Illinois Press, 1990.

Greider, W. *Who Will Tell the People: The Betrayal of American Democracy*. New York: Simon & Schuster, 1992.

Hendricks, M. "Making a Splash: Reporting Evaluation Results Effectively." In J. S. Wholey, H. P. Hatry, and K. E. Newcomer (eds.), *Handbook of Practical Program Evaluation*. San Francisco: Jossey-Bass, 1994.

Johnson, J., and Immerwahr, J. *First Things First: What Americans Expect from the Public Schools*. New York: Public Agenda, 1994.

Kull, S. *Fighting Poverty in America: A Study of American Public Attitudes*. Washington, D.C.: Center for the Study of Policy Attitudes, 1994.

MacDonald, J. B., "Evaluation and the Control of Education." In D. Tawney (ed.), *Curriculum Evaluation Today: Trends and Implications*. School Council Research Studies. London: Macmillan, 1976.

Rossi, P. H., and Freeman, H. E., *Evaluation: A Systematic Approach*. (5th ed.) Newbury Park, Calif.: Sage, 1993.

Shadish, W. R., Cook, T. D., and Leviton, L. C. *Foundations of Program Evaluation: Theories of Practice*. Newbury Park, Calif.: Sage, 1991.

Smith, T. W. "That Which We Call Welfare by Any Other Name Would Smell Sweeter: An Analysis of the Impact of Question Wording on Response Patterns." *Public Opinion Quarterly*, 1987, *51*, 75–83.

Szanton, P. L. "The Remarkable 'Quango': Knowledge, Politics, and Welfare Reform." *Journal of Policy Analysis and Management*, 1991, *10*, 590–602.

GARY T. HENRY directs the Applied Research Center at Georgia State University.

Attention to multiple forms of error can improve the effectiveness of surveys in evaluation.

Sources of Survey Error: Implications for Evaluation Studies

Marc T. Braverman

Surveys constitute one of the most important data collection tools available in evaluation. For example, sample surveys are used to gauge public opinion in policy research and are used with specialized target populations in needs assessment studies. Self-administered survey questionnaires are used in classroom settings to assess differences between program participants and control groups. Structured survey interviews are used to assess the effectiveness of clinical treatments. Surveys are used in longitudinal studies to track long-term change in targeted populations. Although these examples differ in many ways, they all share a focus on direct questioning, in a variety of manifestations, to learn about people—their behaviors, their attitudes, and other aspects of their lives.

Much of the focus in this volume is on sample surveys, which use systematic procedures for selecting probability samples from populations. Program evaluators probably use sample surveys a good deal more now than in years past, due to recent developments that often identify entire communities as program targets. These developments include greater attention to media campaigns as a form of social program (for example, Flay, Kessler, and Utts, 1991) and the current trend toward comprehensive communitywide interventions (for example, Jackson, Altman, Howard-Pitney, and Farquhar, 1989). Randomized population surveys have been used in the evaluations of several

I thank Robert Groves for his valuable and insightful comments on an earlier draft of this chapter.

nationally prominent community health intervention projects, such as the Minnesota Heart Health Program (Luepker and others, 1994) and the National Cancer Institute's COMMIT trials (COMMIT Research Group, 1995). Nevertheless, as Henry points out in Chapter One, the potential of population surveys in evaluation research remains largely untapped, and he suggests that surveys can be used to provide context for evaluation recommendations and to communicate information to the public.

Many program evaluations, particularly those that involve experimental or quasi-experimental designs, do not use population surveys, and their selection criteria for including individuals as participants do not incorporate the technical issues related to sampling from a larger population. However, all evaluations that use questionnaires in any form can benefit from the current research regarding measurement errors, that is, errors of observation that involve the interviewer, respondent, instrument, or mode. My aim in this chapter is to provide a brief overview of some recent advances in survey research, within the context of different kinds of survey error and with particular attention to the applicability of the findings for program evaluation. I have drawn on my own area of evaluation work for examples; thus, most of them concern health promotion programs and educational programs.

Components of Survey Error

Groves (1989) presents a schematic model of survey error attributable to survey design features, which builds on formulations of *total survey error* by Kish (1965) and Andersen, Kasper, Frankel, and Associates (1979). In these models, the mean square error—the total error associated with a survey statistic—consists of two major families of subcomponents: error due to statistical variance and error due to bias. *Variance error* arises from the unavoidable variability in the target statistic across samples of the population units or, more generally, from any aspect of the survey design that will vary over replications. Thus, variability will be found across individuals within the population (which produces sampling error), across responses from a single individual to the same question or set of questions (which produces levels of test-retest reliability), across test items sampled from a content domain (which produces levels of parallel forms reliability), and so on. These error components have an expected value of zero, that is, they are unbiased with respect to the population parameter being estimated. By contrast, *bias* refers to fixed error components that are specific to a particular survey design and leads to sample statistics that can be expected to differ from their respective population parameters by some nonzero, though typically unknown, amount.

Researchers seek to minimize variance error and to eliminate bias error within the constraints of acceptable research costs (see Groves, 1989). In addition, researchers typically seek also to assess the extent of both kinds of error in their data and to calculate what effects these may have on the statistical estimates. Postsurvey procedures can then be applied to compensate for the estimated levels of error.

Within the respective sets of error due to variance and error due to bias, Groves (1989) distinguishes further between *errors of nonobservation* and *errors of observation*.[1] The first category includes errors due to coverage, nonresponse, and sampling. The second category includes errors due to interviewers, respondents, instruments, and modes. This model frames the discussion that follows.

Errors of Nonobservation

Broadly speaking, errors of nonobservation are due to the fact that measurements on some eligible persons have not been made. This occurs when some persons are not identified prior to sampling (coverage error), when some persons refuse to be interviewed or cannot be reached (nonresponse error), and when—as is inherent in the concept of sampling—some persons are excluded from the selected sample (sampling error).

Coverage Errors. Coverage errors arise because units of the target population that should be eligible for the survey have not been included in the sampling frame. To illustrate: one of the most widely appreciated examples of coverage error is the fact that general population surveys conducted by telephone exclude households that do not have telephone service. This is a particular concern in surveys of populations known to have relatively high proportions of nontelephone households, including low-income populations and rural populations, among others. Since this exclusion is a fixed component of any telephone survey design, if nontelephone households differ from telephone households on the survey variables being measured (as they frequently do), the resulting error will constitute a bias in the design rather than a component of statistical variance. Poststratification adjustments on demographic variables such as age, sex, and educational attainment are often made to compensate for biases in coverage.

When lists or registers are used as sampling frames, a different problem arises—ineligible target units may be included. In a general population mail survey that was part of a community-based health program evaluation in Australia and used electoral registers as the frame, Day, Dunt, and Day (1995) found that telephone and personal visit contacts with nonrespondents increased the proportion of units deemed ineligible from 8 percent to 12 percent of the register entries. Attempting to obtain an accurate estimate of ineligibles is important for obtaining accurate calculations of response rates, which otherwise would be artificially low.

Nonresponse Errors. Nonresponse errors occur when individuals selected from the frame are not ultimately represented in the data set because they refuse to participate, cannot be reached, or are unable to respond. Survey researchers have expressed concern that nonresponse is becoming a greater problem for population surveys than it has been in the past (for example, Bradburn, 1992). Because of the obviously high potential for bias that results when a large proportion of the selected sample is noncooperative, a great deal of research has been conducted on techniques for minimizing nonresponse and for measuring and adjusting for it. Couper and Groves (see Chapter Five) present several theoretical perspectives that address why contacted individuals might either grant or refuse a survey request, and they examine those perspectives in light of data from the U.S. Census and several national surveys.

Response Rates. Survey researchers have long been interested in refinements of procedures to maximize response rates. This interest may be greatest in the case of mailed questionnaires, since difficulty in obtaining high response is seen as the greatest weakness of this survey mode as compared to telephone or personal interview modes. The most comprehensive set of recommendations for maximizing mail response rates is probably Dillman's (1978) Total Design Method. In addition, numerous research reviews on factors affecting mail survey response rates have appeared in recent years (for example, Church, 1993; Fox, Crask, and Kim, 1988; Yammarino, Skinner, and Childers, 1991). Factors consistently found to predict higher response rates include repeated contacts (preliminary notification and follow-ups), monetary incentives, inclusion of a postage-paid return envelope, certain types of cover letter appeals, and a questionnaire length of four pages or less (Yammarino, Skinner, and Childers, 1991). For survey projects that use household interview and telephone interview modes, detailed practical advice on maximizing response rates can be found in Morton-Williams (1993).

Adjusting for Nonresponse Bias. Apart from maximizing respondent cooperation, researchers need methods to estimate the degree of nonresponse bias and make adjustments in their sample statistics. Groves (1989) provides technical treatments of statistical adjustment approaches, including weighting procedures to adjust for nonresponding individuals and households, and imputation procedures to estimate values of missing items. One perennial problem for survey researchers is determining the source of information that will serve as the basis for nonresponse estimates. Lin and Schaeffer (1995) analyze two competing hypotheses about survey nonparticipants that are often used to guide estimation measures. The first assumes that nonparticipants are similar to late responders and, in fact, fall at the end of a "continuum of resistance"; thus, estimates of nonresponse bias are derived from the data collected from late responders. The second hypothesis assumes that there are distinct categories of nonparticipants, such as refusers and hard-to-contact individuals; estimates for refusers are derived from the number of temporary refusers (those who finally did participate), and estimates for the hard to contact are derived from participants who were reached only after several callback attempts. However, Lin and Schaeffer conclude that neither model is entirely sufficient to provide a suitable estimate of bias.

Access to Respondents. In addition to the behavioral trends regarding survey refusals, new obstacles to gaining access to respondents have resulted from a number of technological developments. The most significant of these is probably the telephone answering machine. Some researchers have concluded that answering machines do not, as yet, constitute a serious problem for survey research (Oldendick and Link, 1994; Xu, Bates, and Schweitzer, 1993). But the possibility of serious bias is introduced if answering machines restrict access to some segments of the population in comparison with others. This was, in fact, found by Oldendick and Link, who reported that households using answering machines to screen unwanted calls tend to be characterized by higher family income and higher levels of education. However, Xu, Bates, and Schweitzer found that households with answering machines were *more* likely to complete an interview. They also found that leaving messages resulted in higher ultimate participation rates for households with machines, perhaps by performing a function similar to the use of advance letters. Most researchers studying this topic believe that answering machines may well become a greater threat to survey research in the future, due to sharp increases in recent years in the number of households owning machines and using them to screen calls.

Sampling Errors. Sampling errors occur because the elements of the frame population (that is, the respondents) differ on the variable of interest, and different samples selected according to the sampling design will include different combinations of those population elements. If other kinds of error (coverage, nonresponse, and observational errors) do not exist, the difference between any given sample statistic and the statistic's true population value will constitute sampling error. As Groves (1989, chap. 6) states, most statistical work on sampling error concerns errors of *variance*. Certain sampling designs (for example, those involving stratification) are more efficient than others (for example, simple random sampling) in reducing error. However, the danger of sampling *bias* also exists when selection procedures are incorrectly applied in systematic ways or when some individuals in the sampling frame have a zero chance of selection, as occurs in nonprobability or quota samples. Henry (1990) provides a practical overview of sampling approaches that can be used in research planning.

Sampling error is probably the most well studied of all of the different forms of error, and a good deal of effort is expended in survey designs to control it. It has received this attention because it is susceptible to control through statistical estimation procedures, and design alternatives can be developed that yield projections of both precision and cost (Groves, 1989). For example, as Groves notes, almost all major surveys use sampling designs that include complex procedures to reduce either sampling error or research costs (procedures such as stratification, clustering, and unequal probabilities of selection). The other forms of survey error are not so easily predicted, measured, or controlled, but in recent years, researchers have begun to energetically address these other design problems that are more resistant to solution.

Errors of Observation

Errors of observation—also referred to by Groves (1989, p. 295) as "measurement errors"—are due to the fact that recorded measurements do not reflect the true values of the variables they represent. Such discrepancies are caused by factors residing in the interviewer, the respondent, the wording or organization of the instrument, and the mode of survey administration.

Interviewer Errors. Interviewer errors are due to the effects of individual interviewers in telephone and face-to-face surveys. Stokes and Yeh (1988) specify four reasons why such interviewer effects may occur. First, interviewers may be careless or negligent in following directions and protocols. Second, they may have vocal characteristics or personal mannerisms that affect respondents' answers. Third, their demographic characteristics, such as race, age, and sex, may affect the answers of some respondents. Indeed, a good deal of investigation has focused on the potential biases arising from fixed interviewer characteristics such as gender (Kane and Macaulay, 1993) and vocal characteristics (Oksenberg and Cannell, 1988). Fourth, interviewers may vary in their production of nonresponse, in terms of both overall nonresponse levels and types of persons who refuse their requests to participate. The first three reasons are types of measurement errors; the fourth is an indirect influence of interviewers on total error through their contributions to patterns of nonobservation.

The issue of interviewer-related error has drawn considerable attention from survey researchers, but apart from pointing out the need for thorough interviewer preparation, the evaluation literature has virtually ignored the topic. (One welcome exception is provided by Catania and others, 1990, who, within the context of AIDS prevention programs, discuss the evidence for face-to-face interviewer gender effects on reports of sexual behavior.) There are probably several reasons for this lack of attention, including the facts that few program evaluation projects use a large number of interviewers for data collection and that the size of interviewer effects in a data set is very difficult to estimate if interviewers have not been treated as a randomly assigned independent variable.

Respondent Errors. Respondent errors are due to processes or characteristics inherent in the respondent. In unbiased form, they consist of inconsistency or unreliability in responding. Biases in respondent error can be introduced by such factors as deliberate misreporting, the activation of response sets (such as social desirability; see Chapter Four by Dillman and his colleagues), motivational states, and characteristic kinds of memory retrieval errors for a particular task.

Much of the research on respondent error is informed by cognitive psychological models of the processes that come into play when people answer questions (for example, Sudman, Bradburn, and Schwarz, 1996). The attempt to link survey design with findings from cognitive psychology has been one of the most robust and important directions in survey research since the early 1980s. (See Jobe and Mingay, 1991, for a historical perspective.) Only a few examples can be cited here.

One line of investigation concerns human memory for autobiographical information (Schwarz and Sudman, 1994). For example, Blair and Ganesh (1991) investigated the differences among three different ways to ask about past events: *absolute frequency measures* ("During the past year, how many times did you charge a purchase to your account?"), *rate of frequency measures* ("During the past year, about how often did you charge purchases to your account?"), and *interval-based frequency measures* ("When was the last time you charged a purchase to your account?"). Although these variations on a single question might be expected to yield highly comparable results, results showed that respondents provide substantially higher frequency estimates when answering interval-based measures. One reason for the varied results may be that the different formats are differentially susceptible to respondents' misjudging the time of occurrence of an event, a kind of error called *telescoping*.

Pearson, Ross, and Dawes (1992) cite studies indicating that people's recall of their own personal characteristics at specified times in the past is distorted to conform with their implicit theories about consistency or change in the domain of interest. Thus, when their current responses are compared with their previous responses on a topic, respondents often do not accurately remember their previous status with regard to attitudes (for example, evaluations of dating partners), behaviors (substance use), and pain (intensity ratings of chronic headaches). Pearson, Ross, and Dawes argue that these differences are based on memory distortions rather than attempts to mislead. Respondents inferentially construct information about their past using their implicit theories, which are often inaccurate, as clues.

In a final example of cognitively based lines of investigation, Krosnick (1991) has examined the factors that might determine the amount of cognitive effort respondents will expend in answering survey questions. In Chapter Three, he and his colleagues present findings from a series of empirical investigations that seek to identify possible determinants of respondents' levels of cognitive effort.

The topic of human cognition in relation to survey methods really stands at the intersection between respondent error and instrument error (discussed in the next section) because it relates the question design task to characteristic patterns and limitations of human thought. As the cited research examples show, these errors stem from particular forms of response to particular manipulations of question presentation.

Instrument Errors. Instrument errors are related to uncertainties in the comprehension and the attributed meaning of questions and are implicated in levels of instrument reliability and validity. In its *unbiased* form, instrument error will arise because any single scale or instrument can include only a sample of items from the universe of theoretically possible items tapping a skill, attitude, body of knowledge, or other domain. Instrument *biases* are due to vagaries of question wording, question structure, and question sequence. In mail surveys, instrument error can also be related to options for the design and format of the questionnaire. Several excellent texts exist to provide practical guidance on question wording and instrument construction (for example, Dillman, 1978; Sudman and Bradburn, 1982).

Sometimes, adjustments can be made in the data analysis phase of the research by removing troublesome items from scales in post hoc procedures.

In Chapter Six, for example, Green discusses how the Rasch model can be used to identify poor items by analyzing patterns of obtained response, leading to refinement of survey scales.

Word Meanings. Groves (1989) reviews research indicating that a respondent will answer a question even when he or she perceives it as ambiguous or is unfamiliar with essential terms. The researcher is often unaware of these interpretative presumptions on the part of the respondent. One must, of course, strive to minimize these possibilities for respondent misunderstanding in the design and piloting phases of the research. Numerous examples of systematic inquiry into question wording are provided by Schuman and Presser (1981), among many other sources.

Context Effects. Context effects (Schwarz and Sudman, 1992) refer to response errors created by variations in the order in which response options are presented on individual closed-ended items or by variations in the order in which the survey questions are presented. Dillman and his colleagues (Chapter Four) provide a fuller description of several forms of response order effects and question order effects within their discussion of survey mode differences. In addition, Krosnick and his colleagues (Chapter Three) describe several forms of response order effects and how they might be related to respondents' cognitive effort.

Multiple Languages. The meaning that respondents will ascribe to words and phrasing in surveys is clearly a complex and subtle area that has sparked prodigious research. One can imagine, then, that when two or more languages are involved, the additional linguistic and cross-cultural complexities create enormous potential for new forms of meaning-related error to accrue. McKay and her colleagues (Chapter Seven) describe the experiences of several large-scale survey projects in producing and implementing survey translations. However, survey translation is an area that has, as yet, seen very little systematic research (see Marín and Marín, 1991, for a discussion of some key issues and concepts). Given the growing linguistic diversity of industrialized societies all over the world, survey translation will undoubtedly become a more important topic of research in years to come.

Sensitive Items. Sensitive items, that is, items on which respondents are likely to feel a degree of personal threat (see Lee, 1993), pose a particular problem in that the likelihood of bias is high. Recognition of this possibility is particularly important in the evaluation context because many programs, especially those for adolescents, deal with sensitive topics such as drug use, sexuality, or risk behavior. Data quality on sensitive questions is dependent on a number of design features, including question wording, timing of data collection, choice of mode, interviewer decisions, and assurances of confidentiality.

Singer, von Thurn, and Miller (1995), in a meta-analysis of studies that involved confidentiality assurances, found that such assurances improve response *only* when the survey items are sensitive, in which case they significantly increase both response rates and data quality. Mail surveys on sensitive topics sometimes have the option of guaranteeing complete anonymity to respondents through the removal of all respondent identification information (a condition that is obviously more difficult to promise in the telephone mode and essentially impossible in the face-to-face mode), but guarantees of anonymity conflict with the researchers' need to identify nonrespondents for the purpose of targeting follow-up contacts. Biggar and Melbye (1992), in an anonymous sample survey of sexual activity and AIDS attitudes among residents of Copenhagen, Denmark, found that inclusion of a separate, postage-paid "survey completed" card (see Dillman, 1978) did not lower the initial response rate nor did it appear to influence reports of sexual behavior or attitudes. By making follow-up mailings possible, this procedure enabled the survey project to increase its response rate from 45.8 percent after one mailing to 72.8 percent after three mailings.

A particular concern regarding respondent bias on sensitive items occurs in evaluations using experimental designs. In addition to recognizing the problems that bias might cause for estimation of outcomes, evaluators should seek to avoid differential bias across treatment and control conditions because this bias can seriously affect interpretation of program effects. For example, students who participate in a drug prevention education program may become sensitized to reporting drug use. If they have enjoyed the program or feel close to the presenters, they might be inclined to underreport recent drug use at posttest due to a desire to please program staff or to personal embarrassment at having violated newly established classroom norms. If students in the control group feel no such compunction, then differential bias will occur, and the program will appear more effective than it is. Alternatively, all groups of students might underreport drug use at pretest due to fears about breach of confidentiality. After going through the program, the experimental group students may feel more trusting and therefore report accurate drug use levels while control group students maintain their previous level of underreporting. This second scenario would create bias in the other direction and make the program appear artificially ineffective. Clearly, extra care in developing questionnaires on sensitive topics is strongly warranted.

Mode Errors. Mode errors are created by differences in the circumstances under which the data are collected: personal interview, telephone interview, or self-administered questionnaire. Dillman and his colleagues (Chapter Four) analyze frequently reported telephone versus mail mode effects and describe how these might stem from fundamental differences between the two formats. They also describe the extent of the research evidence that supports the existence of the various effects.

As Dillman and his colleagues state, one reason for the growing research interest in this topic is that many designs mix formats within the same respondent sample. An illustrative example from the evaluation literature is the study cited earlier by Day, Dunt, and Day (1995), which used telephone contacts and household visits as two distinct levels of follow-up to a general population mail survey. Another situation that occurs frequently in evaluation studies entails surveying different populations under different conditions (for example, employing group administrations to youth at school and mailings to their parents at home) with the intent of collecting related or parallel kinds of survey information. In such cases, a potential for differential bias will exist due to the variations in setting.

Mode effects appear to be particularly important when the survey questions are sensitive. Both of two recent studies that systematically compared responses to substance use questions across telephone interviews, face-to-face interviews, and self-administered (nonmail) questionnaires found the strongest evidence for underreporting to exist for the telephone mode (Aquilino, 1994; Fendrich and Vaughn, 1994). Aquilino suggests that this finding may be due to respondent confidentiality concerns. The telephone mode offers neither the opportunity for building trust inherent in the face-to-face mode nor the response anonymity possible in the self-administered mode.

Conclusion

This review has been intended to illustrate that a total error approach to survey design strives for a balance of design features that can maximize the validity of the survey data. Undue attention to reducing one kind of error will not ultimately prove beneficial if other forms of error are thereby increased. For example, a researcher may attempt to reduce nonresponse by providing high monetary incentives for survey participation. But even if this strategy results in a higher overall response rate, if it also differentially boosts the representation of different subsets of the population (without the application of compensatory weighting schemes during data analysis) or if it also introduces the possibility of increased measurement bias (perhaps by making respondents eager to please the researchers), the total error will not be reduced, and the strategy will be ill advised. Comparable examples could be cited for other combinations of error as well.

Research pertinent to the prediction and control of survey errors is accumulating at a very rapid pace. Careful attention to this growing body of knowledge will help evaluators to increase substantially the precision of their data. On a larger scale, these methodological advances can contribute to the development of powerful new applications of surveys to evaluation settings.

Note

1. Reference is often made to the alternate typology that identifies the two major categories of error as *sampling* and *nonsampling* errors (described by Kish, 1965, and Andersen, Kasper, Frankel, and Associates, 1979). I find Groves's (1989) model to be conceptually clearer because, as he points out, the term *nonsampling error* is a loosely defined category that joins together such very disparate elements as nonresponse error and measurement error. Groves also notes that although his framework is a comprehensive model of survey errors due to design features, it is not a model of *total* survey error because it does not address errors that occur after data have been collected, most notably coding and processing errors.

References

Andersen, R., Kasper, J., Frankel, M. R., and Associates. *Total Survey Error: Applications to Improve Health Surveys.* San Francisco: Jossey-Bass, 1979.

Aquilino, W. S. "Interview Mode Effects in Surveys of Drug and Alcohol Use: A Field Experiment." *Public Opinion Quarterly,* 1994, *58,* 210–240.

Biggar, R. J., and Melbye, M. "Responses to Anonymous Questionnaires Concerning Sexual Behavior: A Method to Estimate Potential Biases." *American Journal of Public Health,* 1992, *82,* 1506–1512.

Blair, E. A., and Ganesh, G. K. "Characteristics of Interval-Based Estimates of Autobiographical Frequencies." *Applied Cognitive Psychology,* 1991, *5,* 237–250.

Bradburn, N. M. "A Response to the Nonresponse Problem." *Public Opinion Quarterly,* 1992, *56,* 391–397.

Catania, J. A., Gibson, D. R., Marin, B., Coates, T. J., and Greenblatt, R. M. "Response Bias in Assessing Sexual Behaviors Relevant to HIV Transmission." *Evaluation and Program Planning,* 1990, *13,* 19–29.

Church, A. H. "Estimating the Effect of Incentives on Mail Survey Response Rates: A Meta-Analysis." *Public Opinion Quarterly,* 1993, *57,* 62–79.

COMMIT Research Group. "Community Intervention Trial for Smoking Cessation (COMMIT): II. Changes in Adult Cigarette Smoking Prevalence." *American Journal of Public Health,* 1995, *85,* 193–200.

Day, N. A., Dunt, D. R., and Day, S. "Maximizing Response to Surveys in Health Program Evaluation at Minimum Cost Using Multiple Methods: Mail, Telephone, and Visit." *Evaluation Review,* 1995, *19,* 436–450.

Dillman, D. A. *Mail and Telephone Surveys: The Total Design Method.* New York: Wiley, 1978.

Fendrich, M., and Vaughn, C. M. "Diminished Lifetime Substance Use over Time: An Inquiry into Differential Reporting." *Public Opinion Quarterly,* 1994, *58,* 96–123.

Flay, B. R., Kessler, R. C., and Utts, J. M. "Evaluating Media Campaigns." In S. L. Coyle, R. F. Boruch, and C. F. Turner (eds.), *Evaluating AIDS Prevention Programs.* Washington, D.C.: National Academy Press, 1991.

Fox, R. J., Crask, M. R., and Kim, J. "Mail Survey Response Rate: A Meta-Analysis of Selected Techniques for Inducing Response." *Public Opinion Quarterly,* 1988, *52,* 467–491.

Groves, R. M. *Survey Errors and Survey Costs.* New York: Wiley, 1989.

Henry, G. T. *Practical Sampling.* Newbury Park, Calif.: Sage, 1990.

Jackson, J. C., Altman, D. G., Howard-Pitney, B., and Farquhar, J. W. "Evaluating Community-Level Health Promotion and Disease Prevention Interventions." In M. T. Braverman (ed.), *Evaluating Health Promotion Programs.* New Directions for Program Evaluation, no. 43. San Francisco: Jossey-Bass, 1989.

Jobe, J. B., and Mingay, D. J. "Cognition and Survey Measurement: History and Overview." *Applied Cognitive Psychology,* 1991, *5,* 175–192.

Kane, E. W., and Macaulay, L. J. "Interviewer Gender and Gender Attitudes." *Public Opinion Quarterly,* 1993, *57,* 1–28.

Kish, L. *Survey Sampling.* New York: Wiley, 1965.

Krosnick, J. A. "Response Strategies for Coping with the Cognitive Demands of Attitude Measures in Surveys." *Applied Cognitive Psychology,* 1991, *5,* 213–236.

Lee, R. M. *Doing Research on Sensitive Topics.* Newbury Park, Calif.: Sage, 1993.

Lin, I. F., and Schaeffer, N. C. "Using Survey Participants to Estimate the Impact of Nonparticipation." *Public Opinion Quarterly,* 1995, *59,* 236–258.

Luepker, R. V., Murray, D. M., Jacobs, D. R., Mittelmark, M. B., Bracht, N., Carlaw, R., and others. "Community Education for Cardiovascular Disease Prevention: Risk Factor Changes in the Minnesota Heart Health Program." *American Journal of Public Health,* 1994, *84,* 1383–1393.

Marín, G., and Marín, B. V. *Research with Hispanic Populations.* Newbury Park, Calif.: Sage, 1991.

Morton-Williams, J. *Interviewer Approaches.* Brookfield, Vt.: Dartmouth, 1993.

Oksenberg, L., and Cannell, C. "Effects of Interviewer Vocal Characteristics on Nonresponse." In R. M. Groves, P. P. Biemer, L. E. Lyberg, J. T. Massey, W. L. Nicholls, and J. Waksberg (eds.), *Telephone Survey Methodology.* New York: Wiley, 1988.

Oldendick, R. W., and Link, M. W. "The Answering Machine Generation: Who Are They and What Problem Do They Pose for Survey Research?" *Public Opinion Quarterly,* 1994, *58,* 264–273.

Pearson, R. W., Ross, M., and Dawes, R. M. "Personal Recall and the Limits of Retrospective Questions in Surveys." In J. M. Tanur (ed.), *Questions About Questions: Inquiries into the Cognitive Bases of Surveys.* New York: Russell Sage, 1992.

Schuman, H., and Presser, S. *Questions and Answers in Attitude Surveys: Experiments on Question Form, Wording, and Context.* San Diego: Academic Press, 1981.

Schwarz, N., and Sudman, S. (eds.). *Context Effects in Social and Psychological Research.* New York: Springer-Verlag, 1992.

Schwarz, N., and Sudman, S. (eds.). *Autobiographical Memory and the Validity of Retrospective Reports.* New York: Springer-Verlag, 1994.

Singer, E., von Thurn, D. R., and Miller, E. R. "Confidentiality Assurances and Response: A Quantitative Review of the Experimental Literature." *Public Opinion Quarterly,* 1995, *59,* 66–77.

Stokes, L. A., and Yeh, M. "Searching for Causes of Interviewer Effects in Telephone Surveys." In R. M. Groves, P. P. Biemer, L. E. Lyberg, J. T. Massey, W. L. Nicholls, and J. Waksberg (eds.), *Telephone Survey Methodology.* New York: Wiley, 1988.

Sudman, S., and Bradburn, N. M. *Asking Questions: A Practical Guide to Questionnaire Design.* San Francisco: Jossey-Bass, 1982.

Sudman, S., Bradburn, N. M., and Schwarz, N. *Thinking About Answers: The Application of Cognitive Processes to Survey Methodology.* San Francisco: Jossey-Bass, 1996.

Xu, M., Bates, B. J., and Schweitzer, J. C. "The Impact of Messages on Survey Participation in Answering Machine Households." *Public Opinion Quarterly,* 1993, *57,* 232–237.

Yammarino, F. J., Skinner, S. J., and Childers, T. L. "Understanding Mail Survey Response Behavior: A Meta-Analysis." *Public Opinion Quarterly,* 1991, *55,* 613–639.

MARC T. BRAVERMAN is a Cooperative Extension specialist in the Department of Human and Community Development and director of the 4-H Center for Youth Development at the University of California, Davis.

A new theoretical perspective proposes that various survey response patterns occur partly because respondents shortcut the cognitive processes necessary for generating optimal answers and that these shortcuts are directed by cues in the questions.

Satisficing in Surveys: Initial Evidence

Jon A. Krosnick, Sowmya Narayan, Wendy R. Smith

Since the first surveys were conducted in the early part of this century, questionnaire designers have recognized that a structured interview can impose a significant cognitive burden on respondents. As a result, even the earliest textbooks on survey methods (for example, Parten, 1950) encouraged researchers to minimize the time and effort required to complete a questionnaire by using short, simple words with clear meanings in as few and as concise questions as possible. Since these books were published, however, remarkably little evidence has been collected on the parameters determining the amount of cognitive burden a respondent experiences, the consequences of such a burden, or methods to prevent it.

In this chapter, we describe some of our recent work exploring these issues, work that has its roots in the relatively new interface between the survey methods literature and cognitive and social psychology. The interplay between these two scholarly domains has, in a sense, been long-standing, because many leading survey methodologists trained extensively in psychology. But a new era of especially enthusiastic interchange began in the mid 1980s, exploring why seemingly small changes in question wording, format, or ordering could at times produce sizable changes in responses.

The authors wish to thank Roger Tourangeau and Norbert Schwarz for helpful comments regarding this research. Correspondence concerning this article should be addressed to Jon A. Krosnick, Department of Psychology, Ohio State University, 1885 Neil Avenue Mall, Columbus, Ohio 43210.

The natural place for this effort to begin was with *question order effects,* also called *context effects.* Many experimental studies had shown that responses to a question could be pushed one way or another by asking a prior question on a related topic. Because psychologists had done much work on contrast and assimilation effects, they were armed with a set of tools with which to explain such effects, and this effort was quite fruitful (see Tourangeau and Rasinski, 1988).

The focus of the work we describe in this paper is a different set of response effects that have been well documented but only minimally understood: response order effects, acquiescence effects, no-opinion filter effects, and status quo alternative effects. All these effects occur in closed-ended questions and hinge upon how the response alternatives are presented. *Response order effects* occur when the order in which response options are presented affects people's choices among them. *Acquiescence* is the tendency to agree with assertions made in survey items, without regard to content. *No-opinion filter effects* occur when a "don't know" option is explicitly offered to respondents. The presence of this option dramatically increases the proportion of people who say they have no preference on an issue. *Status quo alternative effects* occur when respondents endorse no social change on some issue (for example, "keep defense spending the same as it is now") in greater numbers than they otherwise would as the result of being offered this response option explicitly.

The Notion of Satisficing

In starting to think about these effects, one of the present authors (Krosnick, 1991) came upon a set of theoretical predictions that seemed potentially quite useful: Herbert Simon's (1957) concept of *satisficing.* Simon did not elaborate this concept into a set of structured hypotheses; he simply offered it as a general metaphor to describe conventional decision making. He saw the satisficing notion as an alternative to the common economic assumption that people expend whatever effort is required in order to maximize the profits they reap from their decisions. When faced with a demanding information-processing task, Simon suggested, people often expend only the effort necessary to make a satisfactory or acceptable decision. Thus, people presumably attempt only to ensure that their profits are above a minimal threshold of acceptability. For example, rather than doing whatever is necessary to identify the best-quality car on the market and to buy it for the lowest possible price (a strategy called optimizing), car buyers routinely seek a car of sufficient quality (defined subjectively) at a sufficiently affordable cost.

In thinking about people answering questions in a survey, it seems quite plausible that similar sorts of processes might unfold. Some respondents may indeed be motivated by the goals of helping science advance knowledge or helping an interviewer or researcher complete his or her project. But most respondents are not powerfully motivated to provide high-quality data for these or other reasons.

One indicator suggesting problems with respondent motivation is the decline in survey response rates seen in recent years (Brehm, 1993). Many people are quite reluctant to be interviewed, and experienced survey firms have crack staffs of "refusal conversion" interviewers who are skilled at persuading reluctant individuals to answer questions. It would be dangerous to assume that such respondents are inclined to devote a great deal of effort to answering questions carefully. And even respondents who do quickly agree to be interviewed probably often do so simply as the result of compliance, an automatic "click-whirr" decision that occurs with little motivation to do the job well (see Cialdini, 1993). For anecdotal evidence of this, one need look only at comments written by field interviewers, which remarkably often describe how an interview could only be obtained under circumstances clearly indicating minimal respondent interest (see Converse and Schuman, 1974). When a respondent is interviewed while underneath a car doing repairs or while cooking dinner and watching three children, it is hard to imagine that he or she will expend great effort in the interest of maximizing data quality.

Defining Satisficing. In order to understand the likely effects of such conditions, it is useful first to consider what respondents must do to provide high-quality data. This process, which we dub *optimizing,* entails effortful execution of the four stages of question answering (see Cannell, Miller, and Oksenberg, 1981; Tourangeau and Rasinski, 1988). Respondents must carefully interpret the meaning of each question, search their memories extensively for all relevant information, integrate that information carefully into summary judgments, and respond in ways that convey those judgments' meanings as clearly and precisely as possible.

Satisficing involves compromising one or more of these steps, and it can be conceived of as taking two forms: weak and strong. *Weak satisficing* entails executing all four of the stages just described, but being less than thorough in doing so. Respondents engaged in weak satisficing as compared to optimizing may be less thoughtful about a question's meaning, they may search their memories less thoroughly, they may integrate retrieved information more carelessly, and/or they may select a response choice more haphazardly. Instead of attempting to generate an optimal answer, the first answer a respondent considers that seems acceptable is the one he or she offers.

Strong satisficing involves omitting the retrieval and judgment steps from the response process altogether. That is, respondents may interpret each question only superficially and select what they believe will *appear* to the interviewer and/or researcher to be a reasonable answer without referring to any internal psychological cues specifically relevant to the attitude, belief, or event of interest. Instead, they use cues in the question itself to identify a response that seems easily defensible with little thought.

In this chapter, we focus on four response strategies that might constitute satisficing (for details, see Krosnick, 1991). Two of these strategies are forms of weak satisficing: (1) selecting the first alternative in a closed-question that is acceptable (thus yielding response order effects) and (2) acquiescence (whereby the respondent agrees with assertions offered in agree/disagree, true/false, or yes/no questions).[1] Both of these response effects can be thought to occur because respondents primarily attempt to generate reasons in favor of selecting an answer choice rather than reasons not to select it and because respondents settle for the first choice they consider for which they can generate enough supportive reasons. The remaining two strategies are forms of strong satisficing: (1) selecting a status quo option when offered, because it is easy to defend keeping things as they are now, and (2) selecting a no-opinion option when offered, because it is easy to claim ignorance on a topic.

Regulators of Satisficing. Stated in general terms, the likelihood that a given respondent will satisfice when answering a particular question is a function of three factors. The first is the inherent *difficulty of the task* that the respondent confronts. The second is the respondent's *ability to perform the required task*. And the third is the respondent's *motivation to perform the task*. The greater the task difficulty and the lower the respondent's ability and motivation to optimize, the more likely satisficing is to occur.

Task difficulty is likely to be a function of the complexity and familiarity of the language and concepts involved in a question, the extent of the retrieval process entailed, the complexity of the information to be integrated into a summary judgment, and the ease with which such judgments can be expressed with the response alternatives offered. In addition, task difficulty can be enhanced if an interviewer reads questions and records answers at a quick pace or if the interview situation involves significant distraction.

At least three aspects of respondent ability may be related to satisficing and optimizing. First, optimizing should be easier for respondents adept at retrieving information from memory and integrating that information into verbally expressed summary judgments. Second, ability is presumably high among individuals who have had practice in thinking about the topic of a particular question. And third, people who have stored in memory a preconsolidated answer to precisely the question being asked are presumably better able to answer it optimally.

There are many sources of respondent motivation potentially relevant to satisficing. For example, respondents differ from one another in terms of their *need for cognition,* the degree to which they enjoy thinking (Cacioppo and Petty, 1984). Respondents high in need for cognition are presumably least likely to satisfice. In addition, the more personally important the topic of a question is to a respondent, the more likely he or she presumably is to optimize. The more valuable or useful a respondent perceives a survey to be, the more likely he or she is to optimize. The more an interviewer encourages optimizing by explicit directions requesting careful reporting, the more likely such behavior presumably is. The more a respondent feels potentially accountable to defend his or her answers, the more likely those answers are to be formulated effortfully (for example, Tetlock, 1983). Finally, the longer an interview has been underway, the lower the respondent's motivation to optimize presumably becomes, because of increasing fatigue.

The various hypotheses outlined above constitute a series of explanations for the presumed main effects of task difficulty, respondent ability, and respondent motivation on satisficing. Although these main effects may simply be additive, their relations are more likely to be multiplicative, in one of two ways. On the one hand, satisficing may only occur or may be especially likely when more than one of the following conditions are present: high task difficulty, low ability, and low motivation. On the other hand, the presence of any *one* of those conditions may be sufficient to induce satisficing, in which case *optimizing* will only occur when task difficulty is low and ability and motivation are both high. Either of these possibilities implies the following formulation of the probability of satisficing:

$$p \text{ (Satisficing)} = \frac{\alpha_1 \text{ (Task Difficulty)}}{\alpha_2 \text{ (Ability)} \times \alpha_3 \text{ (Motivation)}}$$

During the last four years, we have been conducting a series of empirical tests of these hypotheses, and in the remainder of this chapter, we will describe the initial results of those tests from three studies. The first, a reanalysis of existing data, tested the hypothesis that cognitive skills regulate satisficing. The second study involved collection of new data to test the cognitive skills hypothesis more precisely. And the final study explored a range of possible additional causes of satisficing.

Study 1: Reanalysis of Schuman and Presser's Experiments

Before we could think of beginning to collect new data to explore the satisficing notion, we were forced to confront a sizable body of published evidence that seemed to disconfirm a central hypothesis in the theory.

Between 1972 and 1980, Schuman and Presser (1981) conducted over 130 experiments, each one varying the form, wording, or context of a single question. These experiments were incorporated in thirty-four telephone and face-to-face surveys of representative national and regional samples of U.S. adults and documented several response effects, including response order effects, acquiescence effects, status quo alternative effects, and no-opinion filter effects, on issues likely to be familiar to most respondents. A primary hypothesis tested in these studies was that more educated respondents might be less likely to manifest all varieties of response effects, including those we believe may be due to satisficing. Because educational attainment is very strongly correlated with cognitive skills (see Ceci, 1991), our reasoning would certainly anticipate such a predictive role for education.

Schuman and Presser (1981) estimated the impact of their many question manipulations separately among respondents with low, moderate, and high levels of education. In only a few cases was the relation between education and response effect size statistically significant, so Schuman and Presser concluded that there was no consistent evidence for the hypothesis that education generally moderates response effects.

However, the item-by-item analysis approach employed by Schuman and Presser (1981) may have hampered their ability to detect a significant overall education effect across all their experiments. In fact, the advent of meta-analysis in recent years has alerted researchers to the value of analyzing sets of empirical studies in tandem (for example, Rosenthal, 1988). Using this method, researchers can evaluate whether an expected relation holds across a number of independent studies by combining the effect sizes or significance levels obtained in them (Rosenthal, 1988). The effect of education in any single experiment by Schuman and Presser might not have appeared to be reliable, but pooled results might indicate otherwise. For this reason, we conducted a meta-analysis of their experiments to re-examine the education hypothesis.

Meta-Analysis Methods. Among the experiments included in our meta-analysis were those using conventional procedures to assess four of the response effects implicated by the satisficing theory: response order, acquiescence, status quo alternative, and no-opinion filter effects. In the response order experiments, half the respondents received a question with one order of response alternatives, and the other half received the same question but with the order of some or all alternatives reversed (these questions usually offered only two or three response alternatives). For the acquiescence experiments, half the respondents were forced to choose between two statements expressing two opposing points of view on an issue, whereas the other half were asked to agree or disagree with the first of the two statements. Status quo alternative effects were gauged by asking half the respondents a question with a status quo alternative and the other half the same question without that alternative. Similarly, no-opinion filter effects were assessed by asking half the respondents a question with an explicit "no opinion" response option and half the same question without the option.

We performed the meta-analysis according to a standard procedure described by Rosenthal (1988), using the computer package *Advanced BASIC Meta-Analysis* (Mullen, 1989). For each experiment, we first calculated a X^2 for the manipulation's effect within each of three education groups: respondents who had not completed high school (the *low education* group), high school graduates (the *medium education* group), and people who had attended at least some college (the *high education* group). These X^2s were then converted into measures of effect size (Cohen's *d*) for the individual education groups. The meta-analysis then compared the average effect sizes among the three education groups.

Results. The meta-analysis yielded strong support for the expectation that people with less formal education would be more susceptible to three of the response effects (see Table 3.1). The response order, acquiescence, and no-opinion filter effects were significantly stronger for the low education group than for the high education group. Interestingly, the pattern of effect sizes for the medium education group varied across these three response effects. In the response order and acquiescence experiments, the effect sizes for the medium

Table 3.1. Average Effect Sizes and Significance Tests for Differences Among Three Education Groups (Study 1)

Response Effect	Number of Experiments (or Item Analyses)	Average Effect Sizes			Significance Tests for Group Differences					
		Level of Education			Low vs. High		Low vs. Medium		Medium vs. High	
		Low	Medium	High	z	p	z	p	z	p
Response order	7	.36	.15	.18	2.08	.01	2.43	.01	.49	.31
Acquiescence	11	.33	.19	.18	3.21	.00	3.07	.00	.16	.43
Status quo alternative	6	.35	.46	.44	1.50	.07	1.70	.05	.46	.32
No-opinion filter	20	.67	.63	.44	6.43	.00	1.21	.12	5.80	.00

education group were significantly smaller than those for the low education group and were equivalent to those for the high education group. But in the no-opinion filter experiments, the effect size for the medium group was significantly greater than that for the high education group and was equivalent to that for the low education group.

The two response effects for which the medium education group behaved like the high education group are both presumably forms of weak satisficing (response order and acquiescence effects), whereas no-opinion filter effects are purportedly forms of strong satisficing. This pattern suggests that respondents of moderate educational level (and, by implication, moderate cognitive skills) do have the cognitive capacity to optimize, but whether they actually do so depends on the satisficing strategy suggested by the particular question involved. When a question offers an easy satisficing opportunity by providing a cue, moderately educated respondents behave like the least educated. But when a question does not offer such an obvious easy answer, moderately educated respondents apparently exert the effort to optimize and thus behave like highly educated respondents. Additional studies on the weak-strong distinction are certainly necessary before any conclusive statement can be made, but the results suggest that this distinction is potentially a useful one.

Surprisingly, the status quo effect was apparently stronger among more educated respondents than among less educated respondents. This unexpected result challenges the notion that status quo responses may be the result of satisficing.

Study 2: Further Investigation of the Cognitive Skills Hypothesis

Although the meta-analysis provided evidence consistent with the notion that cognitive skills regulate susceptibility to some response effects, educational attainment is clearly an indirect index of cognitive skills and one that is confounded with various other factors. Consequently, another study was conducted in which 721 undergraduates at Ohio State University (OSU) completed self-administered questionnaires. This study assessed the impact on the use of several response strategies of more precise measures of cognitive skills: the sixty-item Raven's Standard Progressive Matrices (RSPM) (Raven, Court, and Raven, 1982) and three subtests of the Sternberg Triarchic Abilities Test (STAT), measuring verbal and quantitative skills (Sternberg, 1990).

We also obtained the college student respondents' scores on the Scholastic Aptitude Test (SAT) and the American College Testing Program's Test (ACT) from the university registrar's office. The students had generally taken only one of these two tests; however, scores on one can be converted to the scale of the other (see Marco, 1992). Therefore, we calculated a single score for each respondent, representing his or her performance on the mathematics part of either the SAT or the ACT, and we calculated a single score representing each respondent's performance on the verbal part of the SAT or the reading part of the ACT.

Exploratory and confirmatory factor analyses revealed three principal factors underlying the test scores. The verbal tests loaded on one factor; the math tests loaded on a second factor; and the RSPM loaded on a third factor. We therefore treated these three dimensions as separable aspects of cognitive skills.

Measuring Response Effects. Among many other questions, the survey contained sixteen experiments on individual target items, measuring the four satisficing-related response effects from Study 1 (response order, acquiescence, status quo alternative, and no-opinion filter effects) with four items each, most of which replicated Schuman and Presser's experiments or similar ones by other investigators. Eleven of the sixteen experiments yielded significant overall effects (one response order experiment; two acquiescence experiments; all four status quo experiments; and all four no-opinion filter experiments), and we conducted further analyses to see whether these effects were regulated by cognitive skills. To do so, we calculated measures of the frequency of selecting the first response, of acquiescing, of selecting status quo, and of saying "don't know" in response to the items tapping these respective tendencies. In ordinary least squares regressions, these four dependent variables were then simultaneously predicted by (1) the three dimensions of cognitive skills, (2) a dummy variable representing the item's experimental manipulation (for example, coded 0 for one response order and 1 for the other order, 0 for the question form omitting the "don't know" option and 1 for the form offering it, and so on), and (3) interactions between cognitive skills and the question form's dummy variable.

Results. Regression analyses were conducted separately to assess the impact of the three cognitive skills factors on each of the four response effects. Interestingly, cognitive skills were significantly associated with three of the effects in ways that replicated our reanalysis of Schuman and Presser's (1981) data (see Table 3.2). Response order effects were significantly greater among individuals who scored lower on the math factor but were unrelated to the other two skills. Acquiescence effects were significantly greater among people who scored lower on the RSPM and were unrelated to the other two factors. And the no-opinion filter effects were significantly greater among people who scored lower on the verbal factor and were unrelated to the other two factors. These patterns are all consistent with the general notion that lower cognitive skills lead to a greater tendency for satisficing and, thus, appearance of the various effects.

Furthermore, subsequent analyses revealed that nonlinearities in these three significant relations replicated the nonlinearities that had appeared in our analysis of Schuman and Presser's (1981) data. For response order effects and acquiescence, people with moderate skills showed relatively weak effects, resembling the people with the highest skills more than the people with the lowest skills. And for no-opinion filter effects, people with moderate skills

**Table 3.2. Multiple Regressions Predicting Response Effects
with Measures of Cognitive Skills (Study 2)**

Independent Variable	Response Effects			
	Response Order	Acquiescence	Status Quo Alternative	No-Opinion Filter
Question form	.15[b]	.27[b]	.46[b]	.30[b]
Verbal	.00	-.01	.00	.00
Math	.07[b]	-.01	.00	.00
RSPM	.03	.00	.00	.00
Form x Verbal	.00	.00	.01	-.04[b]
Form x Math	-.08[a]	.02	-.01	.00
Form x RSPM	.00	-.05[a]	.03[a]	.00
R^2	.04	.16	.61	.41
N	719	721	721	721

Note: Table entries are unstandardized regression coefficients.
[a]$p < .10$
[b]$P < .05$

showed relatively strong effects, resembling the people with the lowest skills more than those with the highest skills. These patterns further reinforce the apparent value of a distinction between weak and strong satisficing.

Again challenging the satisficing hypothesis, we found that status quo alternative effects were significantly greater among people who scored *higher* on the RSPM factor, and they were unrelated to the other two cognitive skills factors (see Table 3.2). Furthermore, the nonlinear shape of the RSPM effect here matched that of education level in our meta-analysis: moderately skilled respondents exhibited the same strong effect of the status quo alternative as the highly skilled respondents did.

Study 2 Conclusions. Although educational attainment is clearly different from cognitive skills, the results here are perfectly consistent with our meta-analysis of Schuman and Presser's (1981) data. The consistency of the surprising status quo effect results suggests that the observed relation is robust. One possible explanation for it is that status quo responses may have been optimal answers for many respondents and that the most cognitively skilled were most precise regarding the selection of that alternative. Further research is clearly needed to investigate this finding, particularly research that employs measures of the cognitive processes we hypothesize to be directly involved with satisficing and optimizing: question interpretation, information retrieval, integration, and answer selection.

Study 3: An Exploration of Mental Coin Flipping and Nondifferentiation

Our final study explored the two remaining response strategies hypothesized to reflect satisficing: mental coin flipping and nondifferentiation. This study also expanded the set of predictors examined to include not only cognitive skills but also prior thought about the topic (an aspect of ability) and four aspects of respondent motivation: the respondent's need for cognition, the respondent's perceptions of the survey's value, the presence of instructions requesting accuracy, and the placement of the question early or late in the questionnaire.

Measuring Mental Coin Flipping and Nondifferentiation. In designing this investigation, we first had to decide how to operationalize mental coin flipping and nondifferentiation. If a respondent were to implement mental coin flipping, then we would expect little correspondence between his or her answers to the same question on multiple occasions. We therefore interviewed our respondents twice and repeated certain questions on both occasions. We could then construct an index of respondents' *temporal consistency*. It is possible that this index might reflect attitude change between interviews as well as mental coin flipping, but if we find that temporal consistency is related to most of the predictors we have identified as potential causes of coin flipping, then satisficing is a plausible interpretation of our results.

We also assessed the *cross-sectional consistency* of ratings made of different objects on the same scale. A respondent who chooses to minimize cognitive effort by nondifferentiating will manifest a high level of such consistency. That is, if asked to rate a series of issues in terms of how important they are, a nondifferentiating respondent might rate most or all of them as "very important." Such consistency might also reflect genuinely equivalent evaluations of the various objects, but once again, converging evidence across predictors will lend support to the satisficing perspective. Interestingly, this perspective predicts that respondent ability and motivation will have reversed relationships with temporal consistency and cross-sectional consistency respectively, because the former is thought to reflect optimizing and the latter presumably reflects satisficing.

Method. A representative sample of 425 adults living in the Columbus, Ohio, metropolitan area were interviewed by telephone on two occasions by trained survey interviewers, and 177 of them agreed to be reinterviewed and were recontacted approximately one month later.

The first wave of the survey included thirty-nine measures of attitudes on social and political issues, and twenty of these attitude items were measured in the second wave as well (these items involved two, three, four, or ten response choices). Temporal consistency was assessed by comparing answers to these twenty questions during the initial and follow-up surveys. The more inconsistency a respondent manifested, the lower his or her temporal consistency score was.

Cross-sectional consistency was assessed by the variance of responses to items asking for ratings of a set of objects on a common ten-point response scale. Five sets of four items using the same scale each yielded a variance estimate, and these variances were averaged to yield a single cross-sectional consistency score for each respondent. For example, one set of items asked respondents to report how good or bad U.S. relations with four other countries were, on a scale ranging from "extremely bad" to "extremely good."

Various hypothesized predictors of satisficing were measured during the initial interview. Specifically, educational attainment was used as a proxy variable to assess cognitive skills. Prior thought was gauged by asking people how much they had thought previously about the topics of some questions. Beliefs about the value of the survey were gauged by questions asking how valuable respondents felt the survey would be to researchers at the Ohio State University, to citizens of the United States, and to residents of Ohio. And need for cognition was measured using a subset of Cacioppo and Petty's scale (1984).

Half of the respondents were randomly selected to receive a set of instructions encouraging them to think hard in order to provide as accurate answers as possible, whereas the remaining respondents received no such instructions. Finally, the questions were presented to respondents in one of four orders (determined randomly), so that each question's placement was varied (across respondents) from very early to very late in the interview.

Results. Our initial analyses assessed main effects of hypothesized predictors and found a series of them to be statistically significant. We first conducted ordinary least squares regressions including only the predictors that varied between respondents (that is, excluding prior thought and question placement, which varied across items within respondents). Temporal consistency was significantly or marginally significantly lower among people low in education, people who perceived little value to OSU researchers, people low in need for cognition, and people who did not receive accuracy instructions (see Table 3.3, column 1). Surprisingly, greater perceived value to Ohio residents was associated with *less* temporal consistency. Separate repeated-measures regression analyses of the predictors that varied within respondents revealed that less prior thought on a topic led to less temporal consistency (results not shown; for details on this analytic method, see Judd and McClelland, 1989, chap. 14).

Cross-sectional consistency was significantly or marginally significantly higher (suggesting satisficing) among people with less education, people who perceived the survey to be less valuable to OSU researchers, and people who felt the survey was more valuable to Ohio residents (see Table 3.3, column 2).

We then added all possible interactions between the predictors to these regressions to explore the prospect of synergistic interplay. In brief, these analyses revealed some interactions among variables already found to have main effects, and they revealed additional effects: low perceived value to OSU researchers and question placement later in the questionnaire exacerbated temporal inconsistency (in combination with other factors already found to have

Table 3.3. Multiple Regressions with Between-Respondent Main Effects Predicting Temporal Consistency and Cross-Sectional Consistency (Study 3)

	Dependent Variable	
Predictors	Temporal Consistency	Cross-Sectional Consistency
Education	.20[c]	-.23[d]
Value of the survey to OSU researchers	.20[b]	-.07[a]
Value of the survey to U.S. citizens	.08	-.06
Value of the survey to Ohio residents	-.37[d]	.28[d]
Need for cognition	.11[a]	-.01
Accuracy instructions	.12[b]	-.05
R^2	.18	.12
N	161	396

Note: Table entries are unstandardized regression coefficients.

[a] $p < .10$

[b] $p < .05$

[c] $p < .01$

[d] $p < .001$

significant main effects). Also, low need for cognition and low perceived survey value for U.S. citizens significantly exacerbated cross-sectional consistency (in combination with other factors). Surprisingly, item placement earlier in the questionnaire also exacerbated cross-sectional consistency (in combination with other factors).

Study 3 Conclusions. The results of this study are generally consistent with our expectations. Greater education, greater value to OSU researchers, greater value to U.S. citizens, higher need for cognition, the inclusion of accuracy instructions, and prior thought were associated (through main effects or interactions) with more temporal consistency and/or less cross-sectional consistency. We also found interactions indicating that cross-sectional consistency was greater at the beginning of the questionnaire and temporal consistency was lower later in the survey. This suggests that the tendency to optimize might be strongest at a point partway through a telephone interview, rather than at the very start. Our respondents seemed to progress from satisficing to optimizing, and back to satisficing (in a different form) as the survey proceeded.

The biggest surprise in our results was that respondents who felt the survey was more valuable to Ohio residents evidenced less temporal consistency and more cross-sectional consistency. Although this measure was intended to tap beliefs about the extent of the benefits that Ohio residents would gain from the survey's *results*, it may instead have gauged respondents' perceptions of how much value other respondents would ascribe to participating in the survey (the question wording was: "How valuable would you say the survey that you are participating in now will be for the residents of the State of Ohio?"). If a respondent believed that other potential respondents (that is, Ohio residents) would think the survey was valuable, he or she might have presumed that these individuals would invest lots of effort in order to answer the questions optimally. Therefore, the respondent might have felt it was not necessary to do the same himself or herself and might have been more likely to satisfice as a result. This would constitute a form of *social loafing* (Sweeney, 1973).

Conclusion

The findings reported here constitute evidence consistent with many hypotheses derived from the satisficing perspective. We found that educational attainment can be used to identify respondents who are most susceptible to four satisficing-related response effects, though in the opposite direction to our expectations regarding status quo alternative effects. Our second study indicates that the association between education and response effect magnitude is likely to be due at least partly to the fact that respondents with higher levels of cognitive skills are less susceptible to three of these effects and more susceptible to one of them. Our third study documented the impact of additional predictors beyond education, including perceived value of the survey to others, need for cognition (through a significant interaction though not a main effect), and instructions requesting accuracy. Furthermore, the interactions observed in this last study supported the notion that sources of ability and motivation may at times combine multiplicatively in regulating response strategy use.

In light of this evidence, it seems quite plausible that people engage in various response strategies to reduce cognitive effort, especially under conditions thought to foster satisficing. Clearly, much more investigation of these issues is needed before researchers will have a detailed and complete portrait of the processes of satisficing in surveys. But our work lays a foundation to justify such efforts in the future and, we hope, will help to promote a better understanding of how to design more effective surveys to maximize the quality of the data obtained.

In addition to documenting the ability of hypothesized antecedents to predict which respondents will implement particular response strategies under particular circumstances, future research should also seek to document the cognitive processes through which satisficing occurs. This is likely to be difficult, for a few reasons. Most importantly, the interpersonal dynamic of satisficing involves deception by the respondent: presenting an image of himself or herself to the interviewer and/or researcher as providing reasonably accurate answers, yet not doing the cognitive work that would be required to actually do so. Consequently, researchers cannot hope that respondents will openly inform them about these cognitive processes. Sophisticated methodologies will be required to get behind the self-presentational curtain and to illuminate the processes unfolding there.

Although it is probably premature to offer strong suggestions regarding optimal survey design, some possibilities do seem plausible at this point. Most generally, if satisficing does indeed compromise data quality, then survey designers will want to maximize respondent motivation and minimize task difficulty. Respondent ability and some aspects of motivation (for example, need for cognition) are presumably not subject to manipulation via a questionnaire, so they offer less promise as handles for good questionnaire design. But motivation can presumably be enhanced somewhat by providing instructions requesting accuracy and by informing respondents why a survey is valuable and how its results will be used constructively. Inducing accountability (Tetlock, 1983) by asking people to justify their answers every so often may also enhance motivation. Task difficulty can presumably be reduced by such techniques as decomposing questions requiring complex mental processes into simpler questions, each requiring less intensive effort (see, for example, Krosnick and Berent, 1993). And, of course, minimizing the difficulty and unfamiliarity of the language and grammatical structures used in questions and answer choices seems likely to minimize task difficulty. Krosnick (1991) outlined these and other such strategies in more detail, and the studies reviewed here suggest that such strategies may well be worth implementing.

Our focus here has been on questions measuring attitudes and beliefs. Yet there is every reason to believe that satisficing will be manifest when respondents are answering questions about past behavior, factual knowledge, and other constructs regularly measured in surveys as well. Indeed, it seems quite plausible that when answering a question about visits to a doctor, for example, a satisficing respondent might choose to select the first plausible response option, to agree with an assertion or simply to say "don't know," just as he or she would in answering an attitude question. This logic suggests that the same satisficing-relevant handles for improving the quality of attitudinal data may also improve data quality for other questions, and this logic encourages future research on satisficing in these other domains as well.

Finally, in the face of increasing reliance on telephone interviewing in survey research, our logic suggests a possible benefit of the (perhaps) dying art of face-to-face interviewing. Respondents presumably feel more genuine interpersonal connection with interviewers in their homes, as opposed to interviewers with whom they interact more minimally via telephones. Consequently, respondent motivation to optimize may be significantly higher in face-to-face interviews, thus maximizing data quality. Most studies of response effects have involved telephone interviewing (for example, Schuman and Presser, 1981), and few comparisons of response effects in telephone and face-to-face surveys have been conducted (see Chapter Four). Yet our research may ultimately form a basis for recommending that the costs and inconveniences of face-to-face interviewing may be well worthwhile in terms of data quality.

Note

1. One can also imagine that acquiescence might represent a strong form of satisficing, where respondents might choose to agree with any assertion without thinking about its merits in the least. However, our initial suspicion was that acquiescence is most often the result of minimal, confirmatory-biased evaluation of the stimulus question, and the data we describe are consistent with that presumption.

References

Brehm, J. *The Phantom Respondents*. Ann Arbor: University of Michigan Press, 1993.

Cacioppo, J. T., and Petty, R. E. "The Need for Cognition: Relationship to Attitudinal Processes." In R. McGlynn, J. Maddux, C. Stoltenberg, and J. Harvey (eds.), *Social Perception in Clinical and Counseling Psychology*. Lubbock: Texas Tech Press, 1984.

Cannell, C. F., Miller, P. V., and Oksenberg, L. "Research on Interviewing Techniques." In S. Leinhardt (ed.), *Sociological Methodology 1981*. San Francisco: Jossey-Bass, 1981.

Ceci, S. J. "How Much Does Schooling Influence General Intelligence and Its Cognitive Components? A Reassessment of the Evidence." *Developmental Psychology*, 1991, *27*, 703–722.

Cialdini, R. B. *Influence: Science and Practice*. (3rd ed.) New York: HarperCollins, 1993.

Converse, J. M., and Schuman, H. *Conversations at Random: Survey Research as Interviewers See It*. New York: Wiley, 1974.

Judd, C. M., and McClelland, G. H. *Data Analysis: A Model-Comparison Approach*. San Diego: Harcourt Brace Jovanovich, 1989.

Krosnick, J. A. "Response Strategies for Coping with the Cognitive Demands of Attitude Measures in Surveys." *Applied Cognitive Psychology*, 1991, *5*, 213–236.

Krosnick, J. A., and Berent, M. K. "Comparisons of Party Identification and Policy Preferences: The Impact of Survey Question Format." *American Journal of Political Science*, 1993, *37*, 941–964.

Marco, G. L. *Methods Used to Establish Score Comparability on the Enhanced ACT Assessment and the SAT*. New York: College Entrance Examination Board, 1992. (ED 350 337)

Mullen, B. *Advanced BASIC Meta-Analysis*. Hillsdale, N.J.: Erlbaum, 1989.

Parten, M. B. *Surveys, Polls, and Samples: Practical Procedures*. New York: HarperCollins, 1950.

Raven, J. C., Court, J. H., and Raven, J. *A Manual for Raven's Progressive Matrices and Vocabulary Tests*. San Antonio, Tex.: The Psychological Corporation, 1982.

Rosenthal, R. *Meta-Analytic Procedures for Social Research*. Newbury Park, Calif.: Sage, 1988.

Schuman, H., and Presser, S. *Questions and Answers in Attitude Surveys: Experiments on Question Form, Wording, and Context*. San Diego: Academic Press, 1981.

Simon, H. A. *Models of Man*. New York: Wiley, 1957.

Sternberg, R. J. "T and T Is an Explosive Combination: Technology and Testing." *Educational Psychologist*, 1990, *23*, 201–222.

Sweeney, J. "An Experimental Investigation of the Free Rider Problem." *Social Science Research*, 1973, *2*, 277–292.

Tetlock, P. "Accountability and the Perseverance of First Impressions." *Social Psychology Quarterly*, 1983, *46*, 285–292.

Tourangeau, R., and Rasinski, K. A. "Cognitive Processes Underlying Context Effects in Attitude Measurement." *Psychological Bulletin*, 1988, *103*, 299–314.

JON A. KROSNICK *is associate professor of psychology and political science at Ohio State University.*

SOWMYA NARAYAN *is a research executive with Gallup MBA India, Bombay, India.*

WENDY R. SMITH *is a research associate with the Gallup Organization, Princeton, New Jersey.*

Because people sometimes answer similar questions differently in telephone and mail surveys, the increasing tendency to use both modes in survey designs makes an understanding of these patterns a pressing concern.

Understanding Differences in People's Answers to Telephone and Mail Surveys

Don A. Dillman, Roberta L. Sangster, John Tarnai, Todd H Rockwood

Evidence is accumulating that the answers people provide to survey questions asked in telephone interviews are sometimes different than those registered in mail or self-administered surveys. Although a number of experiments have been conducted in which such differences have been identified, results and the explanations for these differences have not always been consistent.

In this chapter, we review past research to describe seven types of mode effects. In doing so, we integrate what now appear in publications as disparate, sometimes contradictory and confusing literatures by showing interconnections among the likely causes of mode differences. We conclude that there is

This chapter is a revision of a paper presented to the International Conference on Measurement Error and Process Quality, Bristol, England, April 2, 1995. Support for the research reported here was provided by Washington State University's Social and Economic Sciences Research Center (SESRC), Washington State University's Agricultural Research Center, and the USDA-CSREES regional research project W-183, Rural and Agricultural Surveys. A longer version of this chapter, with illustrative tables, is available from Don A. Dillman, Social and Economic Sciences Research Center, 133 Wilson Hall, Washington State University, Pullman, WA 99164–4014.

much yet to be learned about what produces mode effects and how to deal with them in evaluation research.

Evaluation researchers need to be concerned about the extent to which people provide different answers to mail and telephone surveys. Researchers are showing an increased tendency to use more than one mode of administration to collect data for a particular study. For example, a researcher might begin a data collection effort with a mail survey but then switch to telephone interviews for the mail nonrespondents. Switching modes in this way is an effective means of improving response rates. Also, for panel studies, in-person or telephone interviews might be used initially because of complicated respondent selection procedures or difficulty in creating a good sampling frame. However, once respondents have been surveyed and addresses obtained, the researcher may change to the mail mode for the follow-up evaluation instrument in order to lower data costs. To the extent respondents answer questionnaires differently simply because of a different survey mode, the reliability of results is threatened. More generally, to the extent that the same survey item produces different distributions of answers across response categories, questions must be raised about the meanings of answers.

All these concerns make it imperative to understand not only *what* differences exist but also *why* they exist, so that appropriate adjustments can be made in the interpretation of results.

Although considerable research has compared data collected by face-to-face and telephone interviews, far fewer studies have compared data collected by mail with data collected by either interview method (see de Leeuw, 1992, for nearly all comparisons conducted prior to 1990). This lack of research is troublesome inasmuch as the likelihood of differences existing between mail and either of the interview methods seems greater than between the two interview methods themselves, both of which rely heavily on aural as opposed to visual communication.

Early research on the possible differences between data collected by mail and by interview tended to focus simply on whether results were different and, if so, which results were more accurate. This research was limited further by seldom being guided by theoretical concepts, so that the search for differences focused on all types of questions and the interpretation of differences was usually of an ad hoc nature. An indication of this state of affairs is that the one meta-analysis of past studies that to our knowledge has been conducted reported only *social desirability* as a theoretically predicted cause of mode differences (de Leeuw, 1992). Types of mode differences reported in this meta-analysis were response validity, item nonresponse, number of statements made to open-ended questions, and similarity of responses.

During the last decade, this situation has changed rapidly. Many explicitly theoretical attempts have been made to specify and test for a variety of mode differences, and several explanatory concepts have been invoked to account for such differences. In addition to social desirability, these concepts include primacy versus recency effects (Krosnick and Alwin, 1987), acquiescence (de Leeuw, 1992), norm-of-evenhandedness (Bishop, Hippler, Schwarz, and Strack, 1988), extremeness (Tarnai and Dillman, 1992), and top-of-the-head effects (Hippler and Schwarz, 1987). In a landmark article, Schwarz, Strack, Hippler, and Bishop (1991) attempted to bring a degree of order to these seemingly varied studies. They elaborated a cognitive interpretation of how and why different mode effects might occur and related such effects to structural differences between self-administered and interview surveys.

A Conceptual Framework

Our focus in this chapter is limited to how and why people are stimulated to give different answers across survey modes. Further, our interest is in attempts by respondents to provide answers that are "approximately" correct. Thus, we exclude from consideration factors associated with blatant attempts to deceive (for example, a thirty-five-year-old reporting that he is seventy-five). Our interest is in what influences a person to shift categories in questions that use vague quantifiers, for example, "strongly agree" and "moderately agree," often without being aware that she has given an answer different from that she would have given if the question had been asked in a different mode.

We also limit our focus to differences between telephone and mail modes, excluding face-to-face interviews. Except for social desirability considerations, we expect mode differences to be greater between mail and telephone than between either mail or telephone and the face-to-face method. The latter has capabilities for both aural and visual communication; thus, it shares features that are distinct between the mail and telephone survey.

Our reading of the available literature on differences between mail and telephone surveys has led us to suggest seven propositions that describe ways in which answers to questions might differ between mail and telephone surveys and the reasons for those differences. We present these propositions because each has been identified in previous research, not because of convincing evidence that the effects they describe are conceptually distinct or mutually exclusive. Figure 4.1 provides an overview of these seven propositions and of the theoretical mechanisms identified by various researchers as contributing to the existence of survey mode effects. These mechanisms are, in turn, related to fundamental differences in the nature of mail and telephone surveys. The concepts shown in Figure 4.1, taken together, form a conceptual framework within which past research can be described and evaluated.[1]

Differences Between Mail and Telephone Surveys

Three major differences exist between mail and telephone surveys. First, whereas telephone questionnaires require the presence of an interviewer who reads questions to each respondent and records the answers, mail respondents

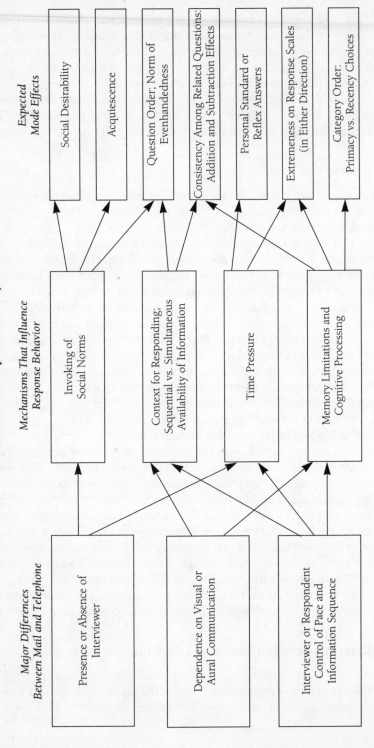

Figure 4.1. A Conceptual Framework Summarizing Factors Theorized to Produce Mode Effects in Mail and Telephone Surveys

Major Differences Between Mail and Telephone

Mechanisms That Influence Response Behavior

Expected Mode Effects

Presence or Absence of Interviewer

Dependence on Visual or Aural Communication

Interviewer or Respondent Control of Pace and Information Sequence

Invoking of Social Norms

Context for Responding; Sequential vs. Simultaneous Availability of Information

Time Pressure

Memory Limitations and Cognitive Processing

Social Desirability

Acquiescence

Question Order; Norm of Evenhandedness

Consistency Among Related Questions: Addition and Subtraction Effects

Personal Standard or Reflex Answers

Extremeness on Response Scales (in Either Direction)

Category Order: Primacy vs. Recency Choices

answer the questionnaire directly. Completing a mail questionnaire can be a private activity, whereas engaging in a telephone interview requires social interaction, usually with a stranger.

A second difference between mail and telephone surveys is the complete dependence on either visual *or* aural communication. Mail respondents must depend solely on what they read in order to understand the questions and must be given written directions or cues as to how and where answers are to be provided. In telephone interviews, there is a two-phase process of aural communication. Initially, respondents must hear each question and comprehend what is being asked. Subsequently, the interviewer must hear each answer provided by the respondent and record it.

The third difference is whether there is interviewer or respondent control over the pace and sequence by which information is processed by the respondent. Whereas a mail respondent can look at, read, and respond to the information on a mail questionnaire at his own speed and in whatever order he chooses, that is not the case in the telephone interview. Although the pace of the telephone interview can be influenced by the respondent, to do so requires respondent feedback to the interviewer. In general, there is a quickness about telephone interviewing; delivery of information is often faster than ideal for retention in the respondent's memory.

Mechanisms That Influence Response Behavior

From the literature, we have identified four general mechanisms that have been thought to contribute to response differences between mail and telephone surveys; these mechanisms result directly from the three structural characteristics that differentiate one mode from the other (Figure 4.1).

The *invoking of social norms* is well documented in the literature and is the result of social interaction that occurs simply because of the presence of an interviewer. Social interaction in all forms is governed to some degree by social norms. These norms come into play in influencing how people answer questions for which some answers are more socially approved than others.

The *context for responding* in terms of whether information is available sequentially or simultaneously differs greatly for the two types of surveys. In mail surveys, respondents see individual questions as part of a larger set of questions. They can look ahead and preview questions that are coming up or even read and answer them in a different order than that intended by the writer of the questionnaire. In contrast, interviewers read questions in a prescribed order and request an answer for each before going on to the next. This variation in context stems directly from the reliance on either visual or aural communication as well as from whether there is interviewer or respondent control.

Time pressure on the respondent for offering her answer tends to be greater in telephone surveys, resulting in a tendency to respond quickly with the first thought that comes to mind rather than with a more reasoned response. The sense of time pressure results from the mere presence of the interviewer, which creates a social situation in which the respondent is expected to speak when the interviewer stops talking. It is further encouraged, somewhat more directly, by the respondent's definition of the situation, in which the interviewer is viewed as being in control of the questioning process and the pace at which it proceeds. To the extent that the interviewer conveys hurriedness because of wanting to complete more interviews in a given amount of time or because of worrying about the respondent's losing patience, the greater the likelihood seems for a superficial or top-of-the-head response.

Memory limitations and cognitive processes refer to the need for the respondent to retain all of the information provided by the interviewer in memory until the most appropriate answer can be formulated or selected. The fact that questions tend to be read quickly by the interviewer, without pauses that would allow time for them to be adequately processed or encoded, makes it especially difficult in telephone interviews for the needed information to be retained until it has been put to use. Mail questionnaire respondents can look back and forth at the question and answer choices, as needed, until their answers are decided upon. Thus, memory limitations occur due to both the type of communication and the interviewer's control of the pace of responding and the information sequence.

Types of Mode Effects

Various combinations of these structural differences and influence mechanisms have been seen by researchers as producing quite different mode effects. Seven mode differences between mail and telephone surveys, stated here as propositions, are discussed in the following section. We also evaluate the consistency or strength of the evidence for each of the described differences.

PROPOSITION 1. *Telephone interviews are more likely than mail questionnaires to produce socially desirable answers.*

A socially desirable answer is one influenced by the respondent's concern over how he will be viewed by the interviewer, according to societal norms. In mail surveys, the respondent does not have to be concerned about how his answer is being viewed by someone with whom he is interacting. Thus, one would expect that respondents in telephone surveys are more likely to provide socially approved answers and less willing to admit to behaviors that are viewed negatively by society, and presumably by the interviewer as well. The experimental research literature has repeatedly found that many research participants tend to portray themselves in the most positive light possible (Dovidio and Fazio, 1992). An early study by Hochstim (1967), in which women in a face-to-face interview were more likely to say their health was "excellent" (44 percent) compared to women in a telephone interview (37 percent) and a mail survey (30 percent), illustrates the tendency to overstate a socially approved answer. Researchers have continued to find evidence to support the notion that the mail survey respondent is least likely to be influenced to give a socially desirable response (compare DeMaio, 1984; de Leeuw and van der Zouwen, 1988). While earlier research pointed to the perceived anonymity and greater confidentiality of the mail survey setting to explain this difference (for example, Hochstim, 1967; Knudsen, Pope, and Irish, 1967), later research has pointed to the presence of the interviewer as the explanation for socially desirable responses (for example, de Leeuw and van der Zouwen, 1988; Aquilino, 1994). Other studies have looked at specific interviewer characteristics, such as age, gender, voice and speech pattern, and race (see Schwarz, Strack, Hippler, and Bishop, 1991).

In general, the greatest pressure for socially desirable responding is thought to occur in face-to-face surveys and the least in mail surveys.[2] However, most of the data are based on comparisons of face-to-face surveys with telephone surveys. There are relatively fewer data on mail versus telephone comparisons, with Krysan, Schuman, Scott, and Beatty (1994) being a recent exception.

An illustration of socially desirable responses appears in Table 4.1. It shows the responses to two questions asked of the general public about drinking alcoholic beverages and driving. The first column shows that 52 percent of the mail survey respondents said they never drove after drinking, compared to 63 percent of the telephone survey respondents ($p < .01$). This 11 percent difference clearly is consistent with a social desirability effect. The second question asked about riding with others who had been drinking, and it shows a similar effect, which Dillman and Tarnai (1991) also attribute to social desirability ($p < .01$).

Although some research has indicated that mail questionnaires do not obtain more accurate information than interviews when highly threatening questions are asked (Bradburn, Sudman, and Associates, 1979), most of the available evidence does provide support for the general hypothesis of weaker social desirability effects in the mail mode.

PROPOSITION 2. *Telephone interviews are more likely than mail questionnaires to produce acquiescent answers.*

Acquiescence is a tendency to agree with others, which, as suggested by Figure 4.1, results from the invoking of social norms. Usually, people find it easier to agree than to disagree in a social interaction. Thus, we would expect acquiescence to be greater in contexts that include interaction with an interviewer (Schuman and Presser, 1981). Dillman and Tarnai (1991) found that in seven mail to telephone comparisons that assessed respondent opinions on how to improve seat belt use, telephone respondents were more likely than mail respondents to agree that each of seven proposed methods would increase seat belt use. Differences ranged from 5 to 23 percentage points in favor of more agreeable responses by telephone, and all differences were statistically significant. A similar pattern has been found by Jordan, Marcus, and Reeder

Table 4.1. Comparison of Telephone and Mail Survey Responses to Questions About Drinking and Driving

Frequency of Behavior	Respondent Reports Driving After Drinking Alcoholic Beverages		How Often Respondent Rides with Driver Who Has Been Drinking Alcoholic Beverages	
	Mail (n = 866)	Telephone (n = 400)	Mail (n = 873)	Telephone (n = 401)
Frequently	1%	2%	1%	2%
Occasionally	11	9	11	9
Seldom	36	27	42	32
Never	52	63	44	56
Don't know	0	0	2	1
	$\chi^2 = 15.1, df = 4, p \le .01$		$\chi^2 = 21.3, df = 4, p \le .01$	

Source: Adapted from Dillman and Tarnai, 1991, p. 91.

(1980). However, in a three-mode comparison, de Leeuw (1992) found no differences among mail, telephone, and face-to-face respondents in the percentage of acquiescent responses, revealing that the literature is not entirely consistent on this issue.

For many survey questions, the socially desirable response and the acquiescent response may be one and the same. After all, the tendency to agree with others is itself a socially desirable response in comparison to the alternative of disagreeing. However, we distinguish acquiescence from social desirability in that for many questions, it is not clear what the socially desirable response might be, whereas the acquiescent response is simply the one affirming the statement or the question. This difference is evident in the above-mentioned data from Tarnai and Dillman (1992), where the shift is consistently toward agreeing but social desirability is not apparent.

PROPOSITION 3. *Telephone interviews are more likely than mail questionnaires to produce question order effects based on observance of a norm of evenhandedness.*

If the first question in a series asks whether the United States should be allowed to inspect North Korean nuclear facilities and the second question asks whether North Koreans should be allowed to inspect U.S. nuclear facilities, one would expect more support for North Korean inspection of U.S. facilities than one would if the order is reversed. The reason for this effect, called the *norm of evenhandedness,* has to do with general social norms of fair play. Hyman and Sheatsley (1950) first reported the effect for a pair of questions asking whether the United States should let Communist newspaper reporters from other countries come here and send back news as they see it, and whether a Communist country like Russia (as Russia was then) should let U.S. newspaper reporters do the same. Respondents were more likely to agree with letting Communist reporters into the United States when that question was asked *after* the question about letting U.S. reporters into Russia. As expected, respondents were also less likely to agree with letting U.S. reporters into a Communist country after answering the other question first. The result is a symmetrical shift in response depending on question order.

As suggested in Figure 4.1, this mode effect is theorized to flow from two of the previously identified mechanisms that influence response behavior, the invoking of social norms and the context for responding. It is thought that the difference occurs because mail survey respondents can read ahead or change answers and thus construct their responses based on full advance knowledge of the context, whereas telephone respondents cannot anticipate what the next question will ask.

Bishop, Hippler, Schwarz, and Strack (1988) provided the first evidence of the norm of evenhandedness operating over the telephone but not in a self-administered situation, using a question concerning the fairness of U.S. and Japanese trade restrictions. However, unlike the reporter questions, these questions only showed changes in responses for the Japanese right to restrict U.S. trade. Differences did not occur when the issue was the U.S. right to restrict Japanese trade. A replication in Germany obtained nearly identical results.

A conceptual replication of Bishop, Hippler, Schwarz, and Strack's (1988) finding was attempted in a survey study of students that compared telephone and mail responses on questions about whether professors and students should be dismissed for committing plagiarism (Sangster, 1993). In this test, a norm-of-evenhandedness effect was observed for both the telephone and mail respondents. Most respondents were opposed to dismissal of the students, but when the professor question—which elicits stronger opinions favoring dismissal—was asked first, the percentages in favor of dismissing the students increased. When the student question was asked first, the percentages for the professor question also changed slightly, but in opposite directions in the telephone and mail survey modes. However, the pattern for the norm of reciprocity was found in the student question for both modes of administration, not just the telephone mode. In all cases, students were more likely to agree to student dismissal if the student question followed the professor question.

Differences between Bishop, Hippler, Schwarz, and Strack's (1988) and Sangster's (1993) findings may be related to question content. While a direct equivalence can be made between the meaning of "limiting U.S. imports" and "limiting Japanese imports," the same is not necessarily true of "students committing plagiarism" and "professors committing plagiarism." Professors might be held to a higher standard than students with respect to plagiarism. Students, because they are learning, might be more likely to be forgiven their mistakes.

A third study of the norm of evenhandedness was conducted only for mail surveys by Ayidiya and McClendon (1990), using the U.S. and Communist reporter questions. Like Bishop, Hippler, Schwarz, and Strack (1988), they found the normative shift in the rights of Communist reporters to come to America and report the news when it followed the U.S. reporter question, but the shift was not found for the rights of U.S. reporters going to Communist countries and reporting the news (although it was near significance at $p < .07$).

In sum, these three studies, the only ones we have been able to locate, provide inconsistent findings. Researchers must await future studies that address the issue of whether effects of the norm of evenhandedness are more prevalent in telephone than in mail surveys.

PROPOSITION 4. *Telephone interviews are more likely than mail questionnaires to produce question order effects based on nonnormative consistency and contrast effects.*

Prior responses can influence subsequent responses because the person is motivated to be consistent with a previous response for reasons other than the norm of evenhandedness. If people have said that they are happy with their marriage, they are also more likely to say they are happy with life in general (Schuman and Presser, 1981). Tourangeau (1992, p.37) describes this as a "carry-over" effect, because information is carried over from a prior question and used when answering the subsequent question; others refer to this as an "assimilation" or "consistency" effect. Tourangeau theorizes that respondents assume there is a relationship between the two questions. The first question has called up useful information for answering the subsequent question. Others suggest that the rules of conversation require the person to provide consistent replies to related questions (Schwarz, Strack, and Mai, 1991).

Contrast effects have also been reported in the literature. In these instances, respondents tend to "subtract out" their answer to a specific first question in a series when answering a more general second question. For example, Schuman and Presser (1981) reported that respondents who were asked first about the acceptability of legal abortion "if there is a strong chance of serious defect in the baby" (p.37) were significantly less likely to agree with a follow-up question about its acceptability if a woman "is married and does not want any more children" (p.36) than were respondents who were asked the second question alone. It has been argued that consistency and contrast effects are less likely to occur in the mail survey format because, unlike the interview setting, the mail setting allows the respondent to preview questions and compare answers (Schwarz, Hippler, and Noelle-Nuemann, 1992).

As illustrated in Figure 4.1, consistency and contrast effects differ from norm-of-evenhandedness effects because they do not involve the activation of social norms. However, because mail respondents are able to see both questions prior to responding, the mail format is less likely than the telephone format to produce differences.

A test of these ideas was included in a survey of Washington State University (WSU) college students reported by Sangster (1993). The students were asked their belief about how widespread cheating was on their college campus and then asked about cheating in colleges throughout the United States. Responses varied depending on the order of the questions in both a mail and a telephone survey. When asked first about nationwide prevalence and second about their school, WSU responses were very similar for both methods. Sixty-five percent of those surveyed by mail and 71 percent of those surveyed by telephone said cheating was widespread nationally. Sixty percent surveyed by mail and 63 percent surveyed by telephone said cheating was widespread at their school. However, when the questions were reversed, (first WSU, then nationwide) the direction of agreement shifted to an evenly split opinion about whether cheating was widespread. Forty-four percent of mail respondents and 49 percent of telephone respondents thought cheating was widespread at WSU; 49 percent of mail respondents and 51 percent of telephone respondents thought cheating was widespread nationwide. When the question about WSU was asked first, the percentage answering "don't know" went up dramatically for the question about colleges across the United States. We conclude that question order effects not based on the invoking of social norms occur, but evidence of differential effects across survey modes is still lacking.

PROPOSITION 5. *Telephone interviews are more likely than mail questionnaires to produce quick answers that reflect a general standard held by the respondent.*

The telephone interview tends to produce very fast interactions between the interviewer and the respondent. It has been hypothesized that, because of this pace, telephone respondents are more likely to complete a quick memory search and respond with an answer that minimally satisfies the response requirements than they are to complete a more thorough memory search (Feldman, 1992; Krosnick and Alwin, 1987). Information already accessed to answer earlier questions may influence the memory search more than it would if the question were given careful, independent consideration by the respondent.

Hippler, Schwarz, and Noelle-Neumann (1989) suggest that respondents who provide quick answers are more likely than others to offer a standard or reflex answer that represents a preformed opinion. For example, people are more likely to endorse positions associated with their own political parties when they respond quickly, in essence giving a preformed judgment. When given the time to think about the position statement, they give more consideration to the merits of the individual issue. The factor in our conceptual framework (Figure 4.1) that contributes directly to this effect is the time pressure associated with telephone interviews.

Dillman and Tarnai's (1991) study of seat belt use found limited support for the idea that quick recall (response to a single question about whether a seat belt was worn during the respondent's most recent trip) produces an answer different from that given when the same question is preceded by a series of three questions concerning when and where the respondent had been traveling in the vehicle. It was found that with the cognitive recall questions, respondents were more likely to say that they had worn their seat belt during the recent trip than they were if the single question was asked. However, Dillman and Tarnai also found that people who had previously reported that they generally wear their seat belts "some or part of the time" were the ones most likely to give different answers under the two recall methods. The tendency was equally strong for both the mail and telephone methods, thus providing no support for the idea that personal standard or reflex answers are influenced by survey mode. This issue is clearly in need of further research.

PROPOSITION 6. *Telephone interviews are more likely to produce extremeness on response scales.*

Satisfaction and concern questions often use an ordinal scale, with response options presented as word-labeled points (for example, "How satisfied are you with your local ambulance service? Very, mostly, somewhat, or not at all"). When these options are presented by telephone, it seems likely that respondents will have more difficulty remembering and using the intermediate categories than they will if all four answer choices are printed on a mail questionnaire. In addition, the fact that respondents are expected to see response choices as an implied continuum suggests that the polar points are particularly important for grasping the nature of the scale and retaining it in memory, especially in top-of-the-head situations when the pace of the interview is controlled by the interviewer. Thus, as illustrated in Figure 4.1, it has been argued that telephone interviews are more likely to produce extremeness on response scales.

Research provides some evidence of such an effect. Dillman and Mason (1984) asked a series of nine questions about the rating of local services, with response options being "not a problem," "a small problem," "a medium problem," "a serious problem," or "don't know." For each of the questions, telephone respondents were more likely to choose "not a problem" than were mail survey respondents. No extremeness tendency was noted at the other end of the scale, perhaps because in this instance, an explicit "don't know" that was not part of the implied scale was the last category offered. This finding may also be a reflection of other influences, as discussed in the concluding section of this chapter. A replication of five items from this study in a survey of college students produced even more dramatic differences, with the use of "not a problem" being on average 18 percentage points higher among the telephone respondents (Tarnai and Dillman, 1992).

Recently, Krysan, Schuman, Scott, and Beatty (1994) reported similar results for three questions asking whether (1) city services, (2) property not being kept up, and (3) crime were "always," "often," "sometimes," or "never" a problem for the respondents. Interviewed respondents were much more likely than mail respondents to use the "never" category. The authors suggested that the effect may have resulted from primacy-recency considerations (see proposition 7). However, in their study, the "never" category was presented last, rather than first as in the above-mentioned studies. Resolution of these conflicting interpretations awaits further research.

PROPOSITION 7. *Telephone interviews are more likely to produce recency effects and mail surveys are more likely to produce primacy effects.*

Some research has suggested that visual presentation of printed scales, including mail surveys, encourages a primacy effect, that is, a tendency for respondents to choose the first answers from a list; whereas telephone surveys encourage a recency effect, that is, a tendency for respondents to choose the last answers from a list (Schuman and Presser, 1981; Krosnick and Alwin, 1987).

The primacy and recency concepts come from the field of cognitive psychology and are associated with memory phenomena. In experiments where subjects were asked to recall long lists of words or nonsense syllables, it was found that items at the beginning and the end of a list were more frequently recalled than were items in the middle of the list (Solso, 1979). The explanation for the ability to recall the most recent items more readily (recency effect) is that at the time of responding, these items are more likely to remain in short-term memory, which has a limited capacity (about seven meaningful units) and quick decay time. In addition, Krosnick and Alwin (1987) have argued that there is greater cognitive processing of the last options by the respondent because of the natural pause by the interviewer after reading a list. The explanation for the ability to recall more readily the first item in a list (primacy effect) is that this item is more likely to be encoded into long-term memory, with greater likelihood of rehearsal without interference from prior items. As typically described in the cognitive literature, primacy and recency effects are separate phenomena, involving different memory mechanisms.

Krosnick and Alwin (1987) have also argued that in visual processing of information, items earlier in a list undergo greater cognitive processing and that those items are used to compare and contrast later items in the list. Again, if the initial option serves as a satisfactory answer, it is more likely to be selected.

However, other research on primacy and recency effects has produced inconsistent results (for example, Schuman and Presser, 1981), and many studies have used show cards during personal interviews as the visual presentation condition, not mail surveys (for example, Krosnick and Alwin, 1987). Until recently, few if any studies have explicitly compared mail and telephone methods. However, a recent project inserted eighty-two experiments in twelve separate surveys conducted in seven states (Dillman and others, 1995). These experiments involved thirty-three mail-only comparisons, twenty-six telephone-only comparisons, and twenty-three telephone versus mail comparisons, on a variety of populations and topics. Only four of the mail survey comparisons exhibited a significant primacy effect, while five of the telephone surveys exhibited a significant recency effect. Only four of the cross-method comparisons exhibited the predicted pattern of mail primacy and telephone recency effect. Thirteen other experiments produced significant differences but not in the hypothesized direction. These experiments bring into question whether this type of mode effect is very prevalent or whether the published literature consists of isolated cases bolstered by a convincing theoretical explanation for the effect.

Conclusion

In this chapter, we have identified seven potential differences in people's answers to mail and telephone survey questions, differences for which research claims have been made. These studies have been characterized by varying theoretical approaches that take into account different characteristics of mail and telephone survey methods. In some cases, the claim of differences rests upon very few studies, some of which have not actually compared telephone with mail responses.

Based upon our review of the studies, we conclude that with the exception of research on social desirability, evidence is perilously thin about the existence of consistent and predictable differences in responses to mail and telephone surveys. In some cases, for example, those concerning acquiescence and quick answers that reflect a general standard, relatively few explicit comparisons between mail and telephone surveys are available. In the case of the norm-of-evenhandedness and primacy-recency effects, conflicting results exist.

Yet too many instances of mode differences have been confirmed to enable researchers to safely ignore the issue. The reason researchers are faced with the paradox of many significant differences yet conflicting findings, we believe, lies in the fact that research has been conceptualized too narrowly. Research has not yet come to terms with the potential complexity of causation and the potential interactions that we have outlined in Figure 4.1. It is possible, for example, that primacy and recency effects are more likely to occur when the content of the question is also likely to evoke a socially desirable answer. Thus, some of the likely causes of mode differences outlined in Figure 4.1 may operate in concert with other causes rather than independently.

For example, questions known to elicit socially desirable responses (questions about the frequency of driving a car after drinking alcoholic beverages, for instance) seem more likely to produce a category order effect if the socially desirable response choices are listed first in mail surveys or last in telephone surveys. A similar idea was recently expressed by Sudman, Bradburn, and Schwarz (1996) when they proposed, from a cognitive science perspective, that primacy effects occur in a visual mode when the first few categories elicit agreeing thoughts (broadly defined). If the first few categories elicit any disagreeing thoughts, they suggest, recency effects will occur. Research to operationalize and test their ideas in field survey experiments is greatly needed.

The proposal by Sudman, Bradburn, and Schwarz (1996), with its emphasis on whether thoughts of agreement or disagreement are elicited by response categories, appears to subsume the invoking of social norms under a cognitive framework. However, people can also agree simply on the basis of whether they believe something is true or false, with no normative aspects implied. Whether this approach is adequate for unraveling the complexities underlying the inconsistent results of past research on primacy and recency issues, or whether a more explicitly sociological conceptualization of mode effects is needed, remains to be seen. In any event, it is important that research proceed on identifying questions that combine as well as isolate various mode effects, and that a new level of survey mode research, with far more complex experimental designs, be undertaken.

It is noteworthy that six of the seven propositions in this chapter predict an effect on answers in the telephone format that is not expected to occur in the mail or self-administered format. The seventh proposition describes influences, that is, primacy and recency effects, that are expected to occur in both survey modes. This finding suggests both a possibility and a concern. The possibility is that by explicitly comparing mail and telephone survey responses, which as we noted earlier have not frequently been compared in large field experiments, researchers have a marvelous opportunity to better understand processes happening in telephone interviewing, which appears to have become the nation's dominant methodology for important surveys. The concern is that precious little knowledge exists on how people fill out mail surveys. Do people hurry or take their time? Do individuals actually look forward and backward so that answers are affected by what comes before and afterward, or do they proceed through the questionnaire once, as is the pattern of telephone surveys? These are important questions to answer before we can properly understand much of the needed research on how and why survey modes sometimes produce different responses.

Finally, the many possibilities for mode differences and the lack of consistently supported explanations of when and how differences occur hold important implications for evaluation research. It seems imperative that evaluation researchers proceed with caution when they consider combining data from mail and telephone surveys. This is especially true for panel surveys, when one mode is used as a baseline and another mode is used to measure change from that baseline. The risk of reaching erroneous programmatic conclusions is substantial.

Note

1. Our purpose in this chapter suggests that it is more appropriate to refer to Figure 4.1 as a conceptual framework rather than a model. We are attempting to bring together in one place concepts introduced by various authors as a means of defining and describing certain mode effects of interest to them, and to show interconnections that have been theorized to produce certain mode differences. Explicitly, we want to summarize past research in a way

that allows us to look at similarities and differences in what researchers have found. A model might more appropriately start with a conception of the process by which a respondent formulates and delivers an answer and the means through which that process is influenced by differences between the mail and telephone survey modes. Our conceptual framework can be viewed as an intermediary step toward eventual development of a formal model that will be based on convincing theoretical and empirical evidence about how people respond to survey questions.

2. A noteworthy exception is a recent study by Aquilino (1994), which found greater social desirability for telephone than for face-to-face interviews.

References

Aquilino, W. S. "Interview Mode Effects in Surveys of Drug and Alcohol Use: A Field Experiment." *Public Opinion Quarterly,* 1994, *58,* 210–240.

Ayidiya, S. A., and McClendon, M. J. "Response Effects in Mail Surveys." *Public Opinion Quarterly,* 1990, *54,* 229–247.

Bishop, G. F., Hippler, H., Schwarz, N., and Strack, F. "A Comparison of Response Effects in Self-Administered and Telephone Surveys." In R. M. Groves, P. P. Biemer, L. E. Lyberg, J. T. Massey, W. L. Nicholls, and J. Waksberg (eds.), *Telephone Survey Methodology.* New York: Wiley, 1988.

Bradburn, N. M., Sudman, S., and Associates. *Improving Interviewing Methods and Questionnaire Design: Response Effects to Threatening Questions in Survey Research.* San Francisco: Jossey-Bass, 1979.

de Leeuw, E. D. "Data Quality in Mail, Telephone and Face-to-Face Surveys." Unpublished dissertation, Vrije Universiteit, Amsterdam, 1992.

de Leeuw, E. D., and van der Zouwen, J. "Data Quality in Telephone and Face-to-Face Surveys: A Comparative Analysis." In R. M. Groves, P. P. Biemer, L. E. Lyberg, J. T. Massey, W. L. Nicholls, and J. Waksberg (eds.), *Telephone Survey Methodology.* New York: Wiley, 1988.

DeMaio, T. J. "Social Desirability and Survey Measurement: A Review." In C. F. Turner and E. Martin (eds.), *Surveying Subjective Phenomena.* Vol. 2. New York: Russell Sage, 1984.

Dillman, D. A., Brown, T. L., Carlson, J., Carpenter, E., Lorenz, F., Mason, R., Saltiel, J., and Sangster, R. L. "The Effect of Category Order on Answers to Survey Questions: Tests of the Primacy vs. Recency Hypothesis in Mail and Telephone Surveys." *Rural Sociology,* 1995, *60,* 674–687.

Dillman, D. A., and Mason, R. G. "The Influence of Survey Method on Question Response." Paper presented at the annual meeting of the American Association for Public Opinion Research, Delevan, Wis., May, 1984.

Dillman, D. A., and Tarnai, J. "Mode Effects of Cognitively-Designed Recall Questions: A Comparison of Answers to Telephone and Mail Surveys." In P. P. Biemer, R. M. Groves, L. E. Lyberg, N. A. Mathiowetz, and S. Sudman (eds.), *Measurement Errors in Surveys.* New York: Wiley, 1991.

Dovidio, J. F., and Fazio, R. H. "New Technologies for the Direct and Indirect Assessment of Attitudes." In J. M. Tanur (ed.), *Questions About Questions: Inquiries into the Cognitive Bases of Surveys.* New York: Russell Sage, 1992.

Feldman, J. M. "Constructive Processes in Survey Research: Explorations in Self-Generated Validity." In N. Schwarz and S. Sudman (eds.), *Context Effects in Social and Psychological Research.* New York: Springer-Verlag, 1992.

Hippler, H. J., and Schwarz, N. "Response Effects in Surveys." In H. J. Hippler, N. Schwarz, and S. Sudman (eds.), *Social Information Processing and Survey Methodology.* New York: Springer-Verlag, 1987.

Hippler, H. J., Schwarz, N., and Noelle-Neumann, E. "Response Order Effects: The Impact of Administration Mode." Paper presented at the 44th annual meeting of the American Association for Public Opinion Research, St. Petersburg, Fla., May 1989.

Hochstim, J. R. "A Critical Comparison of Three Strategies of Collecting Data from House-holds," *Journal of the American Statistical Association,* 1967, *62,* 976–989.

Hyman, H. H., and Sheatsley, P. B. "The Current Status of American Public Opinion." In Payne, J. C. (ed.), *The Teaching of Contemporary Affairs. Twenty-First Yearbook of the National Council for the Social Sciences.* Washington: National Council for the Social Sciences,1950.

Jordan, L. A., Marcus, A. C., and Reeder, L. G. "Response Styles in Telephone and House-hold Interviewing: A Field Experiment." *Public Opinion Quarterly,* 1980, *44,* 210–222.

Knudsen, D. D., Pope, H., and Irish, D. P. "Response Differences to Questions on Sexual Standards: An Interview-Questionnaire Comparison." *Public Opinion Quarterly,* 1967, *31,* 290–297.

Krosnick, J. A., and Alwin, D. F. "An Evaluation of a Cognitive Theory of Response-Order Effects in Survey Measurement." *Public Opinion Quarterly,* 1987, *51,* 201–219.

Krysan, M., Schuman, H., Scott, L. J., and Beatty, P. "Response Rates and Response Con-tent in Mail Versus Face-to-Face Surveys." *Public Opinion Quarterly,* 1994, *58,* 381–399.

Sangster, R. L. "Question Order Effects: Are They Really Less Prevalent in Mail Surveys?" Unpublished doctoral dissertation, Department of Sociology, Washington State Univer-sity, 1993.

Schuman, H., and Presser, S. *Questions and Answers in Attitude Surveys: Experiments on Ques-tion Form, Wording, and Context.* San Diego: Academic Press, 1981.

Schwarz, N., Hippler, H. J., and Noelle-Neumann, E. "A Cognitive Model of Response-Order Effects in Survey Measurement." In N. Schwarz and S. Sudman (eds.), *Context Effects in Social and Psychological Research.* New York: Springer-Verlag, 1992.

Schwarz, N., Strack, F., Hippler, H. J., and Bishop, G. "Psychological Sources of Response Effects in Surveys: The Impact of Administration Mode." In J. Jobe and E. F. Loftus (eds.), *Cognitive Aspects of Survey Methodology. Applied Cognitive Psychology,* 1991 (special issue).

Schwarz, N., Strack, F., and Mai, H. P. "Assimilation and Contrast Effects in Part-Whole Question Sequences: A Conversational Logic Analysis." *Public Opinion Quarterly,* 1991, *55,* 3–23.

Schwarz, N., and Sudman, S. *Context Effects in Social and Psychological Research.* New York: Springer-Verlag, 1992.

Solso, R. L. *Cognitive Psychology.* Orlando, Fla.: Harcourt Brace Jovanovich, 1979.

Sudman, S., Bradburn, N. M., and Schwarz, N. *Thinking About Answers: The Application of Cognitive Processes to Survey Methodology.* San Francisco, Calif.: Jossey-Bass, 1996.

Tarnai, J., and Dillman, D. A. "Questionnaire Context as a Source of Response Differences in Mail vs. Telephone Surveys." In N. Schwarz and S. Sudman (eds.), *Context Effects in Social and Psychological Research.* New York: Springer-Verlag, 1992.

Tourangeau, R. "Context Effects on Responses to Attitude Surveys: Attitudes as Memory Structures." In N. Schwarz and S. Sudman (eds.), *Context Effects in Social and Psychologi-cal Research.* New York: Springer-Verlag, 1992.

DON A. DILLMAN *is professor of rural sociology and sociology, and director of the Social and Economic Sciences Research Center, Washington State University, Pull-man, Washington.*

ROBERTA L. SANGSTER *is survey methodologist, Office of Survey Methods Research, U.S. Bureau of Labor Statistics, Washington, D.C.*

JOHN TARNAI *is associate director of the Social and Economic Sciences Research Cen-ter, Washington State University, Pullman, Washington.*

TODD H ROCKWOOD *is postdoctoral fellow, Clinical Outcomes Research Center, Uni-versity of Minnesota, Minneapolis.*

A theoretical framework is presented that addresses the influence of household-level factors on survey cooperation.

Household-Level Determinants of Survey Nonresponse

Mick P. Couper, Robert M. Groves

Nonresponse is a feature of virtually all surveys of human populations, damaging the inferential value of the sample survey method. With implications not only for data quality but also for the cost of data collection, nonresponse is of concern to both users and producers of survey data.

Two strains of literature dealing with the problem of nonresponse can be identified. First, there is a large literature on methods to increase survey response rates, involving advance letters, payment to respondents, persuasive interviewer scripts, and strategies for timing calls (for a review, see Groves, 1989). This literature has rarely been guided by a set of theoretical principles that suggest the effectiveness of a particular technique, and such principles are rarely deduced from the cumulative results of the studies. The second literature focuses on attempts to reduce error arising from nonresponse through postsurvey adjustments such as weighting class adjustments or propensity models, imputation, and selection bias models (Kalton, 1983; Little and Rubin, 1987). All of these techniques eliminate the bias of nonresponse, under certain assumptions. The fact that such assumptions must be met implies that these statistical methods are based on underlying models of the processes producing survey cooperation.

We believe that both reduction and adjustment approaches should be informed by a theory of survey participation (see Couper and Groves, 1992, in press; Groves, Cialdini, and Couper, 1992; Groves and Couper, 1995, 1996). This chapter focuses mainly on one set of variables needed for such a conceptual framework, namely the sociodemographic characteristics of the household and/or householder. Two steps are needed. The first is to make the conceptual link between social psychological attributes at the individual and household levels and the sociodemographic measures available. The second step is to build and evaluate multivariate models of response propensity involving the sociodemographic variables.

Theoretical Orientation

We believe that people's judgments about participating in a survey are largely made during the brief interactions they have with survey interviewers. Some of their judgments are based on central features of the survey request while others may be reactions to peripheral attributes of the survey request. As Figure 5.1 illustrates, our theoretical perspective includes four sets of influences that we see forming the foundation of the householder's reaction to a request. Those on the left of the figure describe factors that are out of the control of the research design. Those on the right are largely determined by the survey design.

Some of the influences arise from relatively stable characteristics of the householder's social environment or context, which form the survey-taking climate. In addition, attributes of the neighborhood and the urbanicity of the residential location can influence reactions to survey requests from strangers. Also, the likelihood of survey participation is directly influenced by various attributes of each person sampled, such as knowledge of the survey's topic, prior experiences as a respondent, and affective states at the time of the request.

To minimize refusals, surveys with high cooperation rates generally manipulate the characteristics on the right side of Figure 5.1. Surveys that vary in their interview lengths, respondent selection procedures, and modes of data collection tend also to vary in cooperation rates, depending on the characteristics of the population studied. Thus, the factor of survey design forms a block of influences on cooperation. Similarly, the survey design, through recruiting, training, and supervision of interviewers, leads to a set of interviewers whose characteristics can influence the likelihood of cooperation (Couper and Groves, 1992).

The influences of survey design and interviewer characteristics may or may not manifest themselves in the interaction between interviewer and householder, depending on the nature of the conversation between the two. However, we believe that whatever happens is seen through the lens of the social context of the householder and the psychological states relevant to a survey request. In the brief contacts that characterize interactions between interviewers and householders, that subset of factors deemed by the householder most relevant to the decision to participate is evoked and forms the basis of the judgment to participate or refuse the survey request.

Like others studying this problem, we face indirect measures of what are essentially sociological or social psychological constructs, and we need to rely on sociodemographic indicators of these concepts. Furthermore, the mapping of measures onto concepts is imperfect. For example, a sample of older per-

Figure 5.1. Factors Affecting Survey Cooperation

OUT OF RESEARCHER CONTROL   UNDER RESEARCHER CONTROL

```
┌────────────────────────────┐        ┌────────────────────────────┐
│     Social Environment     │        │       Survey Design        │
│ Examples: survey-taking    │        │ Examples: topic, mode of   │
│          climate,          │        │       administration,      │
│         urbanicity,        │        │     respondent selection   │
│ neighborhood characteristics│       │                            │
└────────────────────────────┘        └────────────────────────────┘

┌────────────────────────────┐        ┌────────────────────────────┐
│       Household(er)        │        │        Interviewer         │
│ Examples: household        │        │ Examples: Sociodemographic │
│ structure, sociodemographic│       │ characteristics, experience,│
│ characteristics,           │        │        expectations        │
│ psychological predisposition│       │                            │
└────────────────────────────┘        └────────────────────────────┘

        ┌────────────────────────────────────┐
        │      Householder- Interviewer      │
        │            Interaction             │
        └────────────────────────────────────┘

        ┌────────────────────────────────────┐
        │      Decision to Cooperate         │
        │            or Refuse               │
        └────────────────────────────────────┘
```

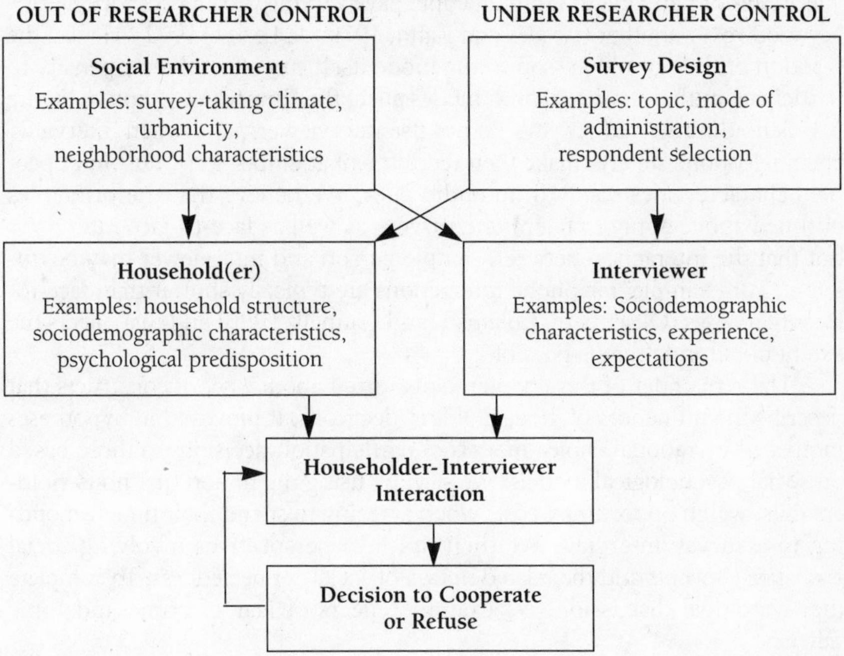

sons could exhibit *higher* rates of cooperation in comparison with younger respondents due to greater perceived civic duty, or the same sample could exhibit *lower* rates due to increased fear of crime. The ultimate decision to participate is based on the combined influence of interacting factors, some facilitating cooperation and others constraining it.

These variables set the context within which survey requests are interpreted. Variables like age, race, and socioeconomic status are useful to researchers in understanding survey cooperation to the extent that they are related to certain shared life experiences. The life experiences of import are those that shape the interpretation of a request from a governmental agency, a private polling firm, or an educational institution to provide private information about persons in a sample household. We hypothesize that the shared experiences of sociodemographic groups produce various predispositions to those requests and indicate features of the groups' current life-styles that affect how they react to such a request. One would expect the effects of these attributes to be specified by characteristics of the request (for example, the survey topic or the agency making the request). These attributes should not be totally causal of the outcome of the request; their effects can be modified by the behavior of the interviewer and the parts of the request that are made most salient to the householder.

There are several sources of differences across survey modes that may affect rates of participation. First, people have varying preferences for one survey mode over another (Groves and Kahn, 1979; de Leeuw, 1992). Hence, the reaction of the sample person to the mode itself can affect the propensity to participate in the survey. Second, modes affect the "Interviewer" box in Figure 5.1. Self-administered surveys do not use interviewers, and when interviewers in telephone surveys make their recruitment attempts, they must infer people's characteristics solely from audio cues. We believe that the principles outlined above apply to telephone surveys as well as face-to-face interviews but that the interaction between sample person and interviewer may be different. For example, telephone interactions are typically shorter than face-to-face interviews (Oksenberg, Coleman, and Cannell, 1986) and that affects the extent of tailoring that is possible.

The remainder of this chapter is organized about a set of constructs that describe the influences on householders' decisions. It moves from hypotheses motivated by rational choice models of participation decisions to those based on social psychological models. We start by using the notion that householders must weigh opportunity costs when agreeing to spend their time responding to a survey interview. We then move to perspectives involving social exchange concepts and the related notion of social connectedness. To complete the theoretical discussion, we examine effects of fear of crime and topic saliency.

Although most of the discussion in this chapter concerns face-to-face surveys, we believe that the framework itself applies to surveys in all modes. For example, societal influences and person-level attributes act as filters to the interpretation of a survey request in any mode.

Data Collection Design

The 1990 U.S. decennial census provided us with a rare opportunity to obtain information on survey nonrespondents from their decennial census records. Using address information available in census records, within the confidentiality protections offered by the Census Bureau computing environment, we matched all nonrespondent cases and a sample of respondent cases from each of the following surveys: the Consumer Expenditure Survey—Quarterly (CEQ); the Current Population Survey (CPS); the National Health Interview Survey (NHIS); the National Crime Survey (NCS); the 1990 National Household Survey on Drug Abuse (NHSDA); and the 1990 Survey of Census Participation (SCP) (see Groves and Couper, 1993). These surveys vary in their topics, respondent rules, sample sizes, repeated wave design, and response rates.

We included these surveys because they were large national surveys being conducted at the time of the 1990 decennial census and because funds were forthcoming from each of the sponsoring agencies of the surveys to conduct the research. Since sample address information for each of the selected cases was used to match addresses to the decennial census, household- rather than person-level attributes are available for study. The number of cases selected for matching numbered over 17,500, with matches being made for 97.2 percent of the interviewed cases (across all six surveys), 96.5 percent of the refusal cases, and 93.5 percent of the other noninterview cases.

The surveys examined here have high response rates relative to much academic survey research. For almost all, more than 90 percent of the sample households yield at least one interview. There are many factors that contribute to the variation over surveys in the response rates, including important survey design differences (respondent rule, mode of interview, length of survey period, length of interview, panel nature of the design, and so on). Therefore, it would be inappropriate to compare these rates to make inference about any single design feature without appropriate caution. Similar caution must be taken when examining other influences on response rates using these surveys, because measured effects of one variable may be confounded with design differences. However, correlates of response propensities that are present over all surveys merit attention.

Because we examined surveys with high response rates, small increases in these rates can be meaningful to the survey sponsors. For example, a difference of merely five percentage points may mean a move from 94 percent to 99 percent, eliminating almost all chance of large nonresponse errors. The sample sizes available to us permitted detection of such differences. To reduce the limitation of ceiling effects, we utilized a logit transformation in statistical models. The analyses described in this chapter are focused on refusals as one source of nonresponse. For our purposes, cooperation was defined as *response, given contact.*

Opportunity Cost Hypothesis

A fully rational view of the decision-making process of a householder would have him or her weigh all the costs of participation against all the benefits of participation, with the outcome of this calculus being a decision one way or the other. The costs would, in this perspective, include the time required to complete the interview, the lost opportunity to perform other activities that are positively valued, the cognitive burdens incurred in comprehending and answering the survey questions, and the potential embarrassment from or sensitivity of the self-revelations that the questions require. The benefits might include the avoidance of more onerous alternative tasks, the contribution to a socially useful enterprise, the enjoyment of thinking about novel topics, the pleasure of interacting with the interviewer, the gratification of having one's opinion valued by those in authority, and the satisfaction of fulfilling one's perceived civic duty, among others.

While we do not subscribe fully to this theory of deliberate and considered decision making by householders, it is important to inquire whether it receives any empirical support. This perspective is common to a rational choice theory of decision making and to a "central route" protocol for assessing the validity of the interviewer's arguments (Petty and Cacioppo, 1986). It is not compatible with the notion that much decision making about survey participation will be based on temporary features of the home situation, peripheral features of the interviewer request, and minor features of the survey that become disproportionately salient in specific interactions. This latter viewpoint leads to the hypothesis that much of the variation in likelihood of participation is explained by the features of the request situation that become most salient to each householder.

This section uses one component to illustrate the latter perspective—the effects of the discretionary time available in the sample household. All other things being equal, the burden of providing the interview is larger for those who have little discretionary time. Thus, discretionary time should affect both contact and cooperation. Those with limited discretionary time are less likely to be found at home and, when they are found, less likely to feel free to participate in a survey. Not only are there societal-level changes over the last few decades (such as increased labor force participation among females) that may be contributing to such phenomena, but there is also individual variation in available discretionary time that may be revealed in survey data. In fact, many of the survey households we approach are telling us this—witness the relatively large proportion of time-constraint reasons given by householders in studies of interaction between householders and interviewers (Morton-Williams, 1993; Groves and Couper, 1994).

For surveys in which a household respondent is sought (as opposed to the selection of a random respondent within the household) or for which liberal rules for proxy responding are implemented, larger households should present a larger substitution pool, increasing the likelihood that opportunity costs would be judged sufficiently low to lead to an interview. The logic of this hypothesis stems from the observation that the tasks required to maintain a household (cooking, cleaning, bill paying, and so on) do not increase proportionally with the size of a household. Larger households share these duties across household members, freeing each for other pursuits. In contrast, for surveys in which a single designated respondent is targeted, a large household may increase the likelihood of finding someone at home who may inform the interviewer of the likely availability of the selected householder (thereby reducing the noncontact portion of nonresponse), but the large household should have little effect on the likelihood of gaining cooperation from the particular individual selected.

Is there empirical support for this aspect of a rational choice approach to survey cooperation? A number of studies (for example, Redpath and Elliot, 1988) report increases in response rates with increasing household size, as we hypothesize. However, many of these studies report bivariate results (that is, they do not control for age, presence of children, and so on), and do not distinguish between noncontact and refusal components of nonresponse.

For three of the surveys in the match study (CPS, NHIS, and NCS), a household respondent was sought for the initial household information, after which individuals within the household were sought for person-level data. In these cases, households with larger numbers of adults would be expected to have greater substitution pools for the initial informant, reducing the potential burden on individual household members. However, there is little evidence of greater cooperation on these surveys within households with more adults (the cooperation rate for two-adult households is 95.5 percent; for households with four or more, 96.0 percent). That is, there is no net effect of more adults on cooperation, in contrast to the discretionary time hypothesis.

To advance the test of the hypothesis somewhat further, we considered that perhaps the total number of adults is too weak an indicator of the discretionary time hypothesis. If we used instead measures of the time commitments of the adults, we might get closer to the concept of opportunity costs for the survey interview. One measure available on households is the number of adults who do not have a job outside of the home. Households where no one works outside the home would, presumably, have higher time availability for the survey interviews. However, the matched sample data once again show little support for this.

Finally, another indicator of a household's amount of discretionary time is available—the number of minutes of commute time and number of hours at work. This is an even more specific indicator of the amount of time at home and thus the amount of discretionary time to give to surveys. Again, we find no supporting evidence for the discretionary time hypothesis.

Our post hoc reaction to these results is that our models remain misspecified and that the hypothesis has merit. Limited time availability for providing an interview will have effects on refusal rates for the subset of cases where interviewers do not effectively communicate their willingness to conduct the interview at any time the respondent might be available. Interviewers are trained to offer such flexibility to sample persons, in order to reduce nonresponse. It appears that most interviewers successfully do this.

Exchange Hypotheses

There are two generalizations and elaborations of the rational decision making perspective underlying the discretionary time hypothesis. One expands the notion of cost-benefit assessments to the perceived equity of long-term associations between persons or between a person and societal institutions. This approach uses many of the concepts of social exchange theories. The other approach observes that some subgroups in the society may not feel the influence of norms extant in the dominant society. To the extent that survey responding is a norm, they might not recognize it. This is commonly referred to as the social location or social isolation theory.

The two approaches are related conceptually. For example, a long history of inequitable social exchange relationships between a subgroup and the larger society may lead to the development of a subculture that explicitly fails to include the norms of the larger culture. This logic has been applied to findings of lower response rates among racial and ethnic subgroups. Similarly, the absence of ongoing relationships between one group and the larger society will lead to the absence of shared norms. This logic has been applied to findings of lower response rates among the elderly (Glenn, 1969; Mercer and Butler, 1967). Because of the conceptual overlap in the two theoretical discussions, we juxtapose them in this and the next section, and will discuss indicators that are appropriate to both constructs.

Social exchange hypotheses have been popular in the discussion of survey participation in the literature (see Dillman, 1978; Goyder, 1987). Social exchange may operate at any number of levels, ranging from exchange in dyadic interactions (reciprocation in social interaction) to exchange relationships between an individual and the larger society (civic duty). On the one hand, Dillman's (1978) views on exchange reflect a rich literature in mail surveys focusing on social exchange within a relatively closed system (survey organization and householder), with relatively small gestures on the part of the survey organization (personalized letters, token incentives, reminder letters) hypothesized to evoke a reciprocating response from the householder. On the other hand, Goyder's (1987) discussion of exchange evokes a wide array of obligations and expectations between an individual and various institutions of society over an extended period of time. Central to all conceptualizations of social exchange is the notion that as in economic exchange, all social "commodities" (ranging from measurable entities such as time and information to less tangible socio-emotional entities such as approval) are part of an intuitive complex bookkeeping system in which debts (obligations) and credits (demands and expectations) are stored.

Thus, virtually any relationship can be described in exchange terms. Whether the social exchange perspective applies to face-to-face survey requests may depend on whether the request is perceived by the householders as applicable to some relationship they have or will have with another person or institution. For single-contact surveys, conducted for or by organizations with no prior connection to the household, the exchange perspective may have value only to provide insight into the influence of incentives and interviewer behaviors on cooperation or refusal. For surveys conducted by organizations with ongoing contact with the households, however, the exchange notion may be quite useful.

For governmental surveys, the effects of social exchange principles or norms may involve the cumulative effect of multiple governmental contacts. The full weight of past relationships with the agency or organization making the survey request (or with the broader class of institutions it represents) may be brought to bear in the householder's reaction to the survey request. Those with the fewest services provided by the government or with the least need for such services may feel less need to reciprocate. Hence, indicators of socioeconomic status should broadly reflect exchange influences on governmental survey participation. DeMaio (1980) found significant differences in refusal rates by income, with middle-income households being most likely to refuse and low-income households least likely to refuse. A number of studies have reported cooperation rates increasing with other indicators of socioeconomic status, such as social class (Lindström, 1986; Redpath and Elliot, 1988) and property value (Goyder, 1987). A gross measure of socioeconomic status available to us is the nature of housing costs faced by the household. When these variables are combined in a logistic regression model there is strong evidence that those renting or owning expensive housing units are less likely to cooperate than others.

Furthermore, to the extent that surveys are viewed as research and information gathering, those who appreciate the utility of such efforts or who have benefited from such efforts will tend to cooperate. This would extend beyond government-sponsored surveys to those conducted by academic organizations and even to some surveys conducted for commercial purposes. Education may serve as a proxy. There is support for higher cooperation rates in higher education groups (Foster and Bushnell, 1994; Kemsley, 1975, 1976; O'Neil, 1979). Our data show the opposite, however. The bivariate effects of education show somewhat higher participation among lower education groups.

A more direct measure of exchange debts owed to the government may be whether the household currently receives any public assistance from a governmental agency. One might expect that those households currently receiving benefits would feel more pressure to comply with a survey request from a governmental agency. There was, however, no support for this hypothesis in the data.

Finally, when we combined these several variables into an overall model for the effects of social exchange indicators, the data did not detect education effects in the presence of the housing cost indicators, which remain influential (with higher cost housing associated with greater refusals).

Social Connectedness and Authority Hypotheses

Social-connectedness hypotheses are closely tied to the agencies collecting the data and to the broader social institutions they may represent. Social connectedness is akin to the notions of civic duty that may apply when the agency collecting the data represents an important social institution of a society (for example, a government or a university). Thus, those who are alienated or isolated from the broader society or polity would be expected to be less likely to cooperate with survey requests that represent such interests. To the extent that large-scale national surveys are tools of the central institutions of society, those at the periphery of society would feel less normative inclination to participate.

Another rationale behind this set of hypotheses is the view that surveys are inherently social events because they describe and collect information on populations. To the extent that sample persons feel social cohesion with the defined population, cooperation will be enhanced. This might be one reason for the relatively higher rates of cooperation in organizational membership surveys. Cooperation in surveys may be seen both as an obligation of group membership and as an affirmation of one's membership.

There are both structural and social psychological aspects to alienation or social isolation. Some groups (for example, the very poor), by virtue of their position in society, may not be bound psychologically to the larger society to the same extent as others. Such alienation would lead, one might assert, to lower levels of cooperation with surveys representing those agents of government. This view equates survey participation with other acts of political or social participation, such as voting. The attachment of alienated groups (often identified in terms of race and/or socioeconomic status in the United States and by class in other countries) to society is believed to be weak, and such groups are posited to be less likely to participate in a variety of social and political activities, including responding to surveys.

This has been a popular hypothesis with regard to the behavior of racial and ethnic subgroups in surveys. However, there is little evidence in the literature that nonwhites cooperate with survey requests at lower rates than whites. O'Neil (1979) found lower rates of resistance among blacks to a telephone survey in Chicago, while Hawkins (1975) reported similar results for a face-to-face survey in Detroit. Both DeMaio (1980) and Smith (1983) failed to find effects of race on cooperation rates. Our own data show lower rates of contact in minority race/ethnicity groups, but the highest *cooperation* rates are among blacks and Hispanics, once they are contacted.

On a social psychological level, some people may experience a sense of social isolation or disengagement from society that may not be wholly related to their position in that society. Some indicators of this social isolation might be whether the household is a single person (those living alone tending to be less socially integrated), whether there are children in the household (those with children having higher social integration through schools and networks of friends), whether the household predominantly consists of elderly persons (following the disengagement of the elderly hypothesis), and whether the household has moved recently (those more transient having fewer community roots).

Findings from Great Britain all point to lower response rates for single-person households (Kemsley 1975, 1976; Norris, 1987). However, Barnes and Birch (1975) found that although single-person households have the highest noncontact rate, their refusal rates are not much different from two- to three-person households. Paul and Lawes (1982) found higher rates of nonresponse among single-person households (but note that these households disproportionately consisted of older persons). Smith (1983) reported higher refusal rates among single-person households, as did Brown and Bishop (1982) and Ekholm and Laaksonen (1990).

Without exception, every study that has examined response or cooperation finds positive effects of the presence of children in the household (for example, Kemsley, 1975; Redpath, 1986; Lievesley, 1988). While Kemsley found that the presence of children has a positive effect on response, the total number of children has no effect.

Contrary to expectation, the findings on residential mobility suggest that higher refusal rates are found among nonmovers than among movers. Barnes and Birch (1975) found that this difference persists whether comparing mobility in the past year or the past five years and whether examining mobility of the head of household or of all members of the household. Redpath (1986) found that those who had moved in the last twelve months were more likely to respond. Comstock and Helsing (1973) also found more refusers among nonmovers.

Our data generally support the assertion that these indicators are related to likelihood of cooperation with a survey request. Single-person households have lower cooperation rates than multi-person households; those with children under five years old have higher cooperation rates than others; those households with some members who have moved in the last five years have lower cooperation than others.

A concept related to social connectedness is that of authority, the existence of legitimized power of a person or institution over the behavior of persons. Cialdini (1984) and others have noted that when persons or institutions with authority over the lives of the requestees seek assistance, cooperation decisions might be made with little attention to the costs and benefits of the task. We believe that influences of authority are important in understanding compliance with governmental survey requests but probably not requests from academic or commercial survey organizations.

In the decennial census data, we examined two indicators: whether a household member was in the military (as an indicator of a behavioral commitment to governmental authority), and whether all members of the household were citizens (with those who were not citizens more likely to be sensitive to governmental authority than others). Households with members in the military do indeed exhibit higher cooperation rates, but there are no direct effects of citizenship on cooperation. Combining the two variables, we found that the lowest cooperation occurs among households with nonmilitary citizens, while those with some noncitizens or those with military members have the highest cooperation.

Finally, when all the social isolation and authority indicators are combined into a multivariate model, people living in single-family units, multi-person households, households with children, younger households (those with all members less than thirty years old) or older households (those with all members seventy years old or older)—along with blacks, Hispanics, and people experiencing a move in the last five years—are more likely to be cooperative. Significant bivariate predictors that are eliminated through statistical controls are citizenship, military duty, and non-English-speaking indicators.

Other Popular Hypotheses

The literature contains some speculations about other influences on survey cooperation, reviewed briefly here.

Fear of Crime. The reluctance of some persons to cooperate with surveys because they fear criminal victimization is a specific form of a script error—the misconstrual of the survey request as an attempt to gain entry and physical access to the householder for purposes of theft or assault. One would expect that fear of crime might make householders reluctant to respond to an unexpected knock on the door and that it might be a stronger influence on behavior when the person attempting contact with the household appears threatening in any way. The common use of female interviewers in surveys might dampen the effect of fear of crime. Researchers have very imperfect indicators to test this hypothesis. However, there is little evidence from our data that women living alone (who might have greater fears) or elderly respondents (who do exhibit more fear of crime; see, for example, Rucker, 1990) have lower cooperation rates.

Topic Saliency. A common metaphor for survey interviews is a "conversation with a purpose." There is much speculation that when the purposes of the conversation are consistent with goals held by the sampled persons, the persons tend to cooperate. This speculation is based on hypotheses that surveys on salient topics may offer some chance of personal gain to the respondents because their group might be advantaged by the survey information, and also that the chance to exhibit one's knowledge on the topic would be gratifying. Couper (1995), for example, found that those who express little interest in politics are more likely to decline participation in electoral behavior surveys. The decennial census data offer few indicators to test hypotheses concerning topic saliency.

Combined Influences of Household-Level Variables on Cooperation

Many of the hypotheses reviewed above are not independent of one another. For example, those socially isolated in the society are less likely to have the normative guidance of social exchange relationships with survey takers. Hence, deeper understanding of the nature of the survey participation process might be gained by combined multivariate analysis of the different indicators. In combining these household-level variables, one needs to control for survey design and social environmental variables when possible.

The analyses presented thus far use some variables measured on all cases and some variables measured only for the one-sixth subsample who received the long form of the census. First, we specified a model that included only variables measured on all cases. Then we fit models that included the one long-form predictor that survived the multivariate controls introduced earlier: an indicator of residential mobility of the household. That model exhibited severely reduced effects of mobility in the presence of other indicators. Hence, we concentrate here on the results from the analysis of short-form variables.

Table 5.1 shows a multivariate logistic regression based on the full sample, predicting the likelihood of an interview, relative to a refusal, among sample households contacted for the six surveys. The model controls for covariates not at the household level: dummy variables for the six different surveys (to

Table 5.1. Multivariate Logistic Regression Coefficients for a Model of Cooperation Versus Refusal

	Coefficient	Standard Error
Intercept	2.66[b]	0.24
Control variables		
Survey indicators		
CPS	1.42[b]	0.17
NHIS	1.13[b]	0.18
NCS	1.62[b]	0.21
NHSDA	-0.53[b]	0.16
SCP	0.38[a]	0.19
(CEQ)	—	—
Urbanicity		
Central city of consolidated metropolitan statistical area (CMSA)	-0.47[b]	0.14
Balance of CMSA	-0.20	0.13
(Other)	—	—
Household-level variables		
Race/ethnicity		
Black	0.34[a]	0.14
Hispanic	0.55[a]	0.23
(Other)	—	—
Single-person household (1 = yes; 0 = no)	-0.31[a]	0.13
Housing structure		
Single-family unit	0.30	0.17
Large multi-unit structure	0.09	0.18
(Other)	—	—
Children in household (1 = yes; 0 = no)	0.21	0.11
Age composition of household		
All < 30 yrs.	0.81[b]	0.15
All ≥ 70 yrs.	0.38[a]	0.18
(Other)	—	—
Owner-occupied housing unit (1 = yes; 0 = no)	-0.25	0.21
Monthly rent for renters (in units of $100)	-0.039	0.031
House value for owners (in units of $10,000)	-0.012[a]	0.0057

Note: Dependent variable coded 1 = interview, 0 = refusal.

[a] $p < .05$

[b] $p < .01$

control on omitted design differences among the surveys) and three levels of urbanicity (to partially control for social environment differences). The analysis shows that Hispanics and blacks, multi-person households, younger households (all members less than thirty years old) and older households (all members seventy years old or older), and those not owning expensive homes tend to cooperate with surveys. In the presence of these variables, the type of housing structure and the presence of children fail to demonstrate significant effects on participation.

Conclusion

Efforts to reduce nonresponse in surveys or to construct more effective post-survey adjustment procedures need more theoretical guidance about the underlying influences on decisions regarding survey participation. The heart of this problem is the decision to cooperate with a survey request once a sample person is contacted. The use of demographic data on survey nonrespondents and respondents, available from a match to the decennial census records, permitted us to test in tentative ways how alternative theoretical frameworks apply to the potential respondent's interview decision.

The theoretical hypotheses we reviewed are supported to varying degrees by our data. There is little support in our data for the discretionary time hypothesis—that sample persons with little available time tend to be nonrespondent. We suspect this hypothesis will be more relevant to the noncontact component of nonresponse. The exchange hypothesis demonstrates more power to explain survey participation. Similarly, indicators of the degree of connectedness to the larger society and of openness to authority perform in the expected direction.

The data used in this chapter come from surveys with response rates that are higher than those typical of academic or commercial surveys. They result from designs that employ unusual efforts to contact all sample households; thus, their noncontact rates tend to be unusually low. Their refusal rates are also low but have some parallels in other surveys. Since the analyses concentrate on cooperation of sample persons once they are contacted, the inferential limitations of the analyses depend on whether the influences on cooperation are different for lower response rate surveys than for these high response rate surveys. We suspect that some differences across surveys in influences on cooperation arise from different design features (such as survey topic or length of interview). These design features do not necessarily affect household-level influences, because they are part of the survey request for all the demographic and social subgroups. By pooling data over surveys that vary on some of these design features, we measured the effects of household-level attributes that are robust to the design features.

Only if some subgroups of the population react to design features differently than do others will the kinds of models discussed in this chapter be inapplicable to surveys with lower response rates. One example of this might be the tendency for persons uninterested or uninformed about a topic to refuse a survey request (see Couper, 1995) or for those who are busy to be disproportionately nonrespondent to surveys conducted over just a few days. For a survey with very low levels of effort to contact sample persons, the refusal cases will consist of those who are easily contacted. In such cases, the magnitude of predictive power for some of the household-level variables may be larger, because their effects will not have been attenuated by repeated persuasive efforts of interviewers. For the most part, however, we speculate that the general form of the models will remain the same at lower response rate levels.

This chapter began with a statement of a theoretical framework for survey participation that if correct should be useful both for design efforts to reduce nonresponse rates and for efforts to build effective tools for nonresponse adjustment. The framework notes that influences on survey participation are a multilevel phenomenon. They arise from a survey-taking climate in the society and from other social environmental forces, as well as from household- and person-level attributes that combine to form relatively stable filters through which people interpret the survey request. The survey designer has a variety of tools to enhance the attractiveness of the survey request, one important tool being the selection of interviewers and the behaviors they are asked to exhibit. All of these features define the psychological and behavioral context of a conversation between the interviewer and a sample person in which the interviewer requests participation in the survey. These conversations constitute the proximate causes of survey response rates. This chapter has shown that even without measurement of these proximate causes, systematic and measurable variations exist across persons and households in their tendency to comply with survey requests. Adding measurement of these proximate causes, through observation of conversations between interviewers and respondents, provides further insight into the process of survey participation (Groves and Couper, 1996; Groves, Raghunathan, and Couper, 1995). Such insight is necessary for a complete understanding of the phenomenon.

A further omission from this chapter is a set of variables related to the specific topics of individual surveys. That is, as noted above, a sample person may accept or refuse a survey based on the survey's likelihood, on the one hand, of being interesting and/or providing the person a chance to demonstrate knowledge in a field or, on the other hand, of being boring, posing a threat to self-esteem, or being likely to expose the person's ignorance of a topic. These causes of survey participation linked to particular survey topics form a set of potential causes that are *most* productive of nonresponse error ("nonignorable" in the terminology of Rubin, 1986, p.22), because the likelihood of nonresponse is a function of the survey variables themselves.

This chapter had the goal of sensitizing practitioners to a theoretical framework of survey participation and also to the need to consider alternative design features to attack various nonresponse weaknesses in specific surveys they conduct. Field administrative procedures and postsurvey adjustments for nonresponse can be improved only if the designer understands the process of survey participation.

References

Barnes, R., and Birch, F. *The Census as an Aid in Estimating the Characteristics of Non-Response in the GHS.* New Methodology Series No. NM1. London: Office of Population Censuses and Surveys, 1975.

Brown, P. R., and Bishop, G. F. "Who Refuses and Resists in Telephone Surveys? Some New Evidence." Paper presented at the annual conference of the Midwest Association for Public Opinion Research, Chicago, November 1982.

Cialdini, R. B. *Influence: The New Psychology of Modern Persuasion.* New York: Quill, 1984.

Comstock, G. W., and Helsing, K. J. "Characteristics of Respondents and Nonrespondents to a Questionnaire for Estimating Community Mood." *American Journal of Epidemiology,* 1973, *97* (4), 233–239.

Couper, M. P. "The Impact of Survey Introductions on Data Quality." Paper presented at the International Conference on Survey Measurement and Process Quality, Bristol, England, April 1995.

Couper, M. P., and Groves, R. M. "The Role of the Interviewer in Survey Participation." *Survey Methodology,* 1992, *18* (2), 263–271.

Couper, M. P., and Groves, R. M. "Social Environmental Impacts on Survey Cooperation." *Quality and Quantity,* in press.

de Leeuw, E. D. *Data Quality in Mail, Telephone, and Face to Face Surveys.* Amsterdam, Netherlands: TT-Publikaties, 1992.

DeMaio, T. J. "Refusals: Who, Where and Why?" *Public Opinion Quarterly,* 1980, *44,* 223–233.

Dillman, D. *Mail and Telephone Surveys: The Total Design Method.* New York: Wiley, 1978.

Ekholm, A., and Laaksonen, S. *Reweighting by Nonresponse Modeling in the Finnish Household Survey.* Research Report No. 68. Helsinki: Department of Statistics, 1990.

Foster, K., and Bushnell, D. "Non-Response Bias on Government Surveys in Great Britain." Paper presented at the Fifth International Workshop on Household Survey Nonresponse, Ottawa, September 1994.

Glenn, N. G. "Aging, Disengagement, and Opinionation." *Public Opinion Quarterly,* 1969, *33* (1), 17–33.

Goyder, J. *The Silent Minority; Nonrespondents on Sample Surveys.* Boulder, Colo.: Westview Press, 1987.

Groves, R. M. *Survey Errors and Survey Costs.* New York: Wiley, 1989.

Groves, R. M., Cialdini, R. B., and Couper, M. P. "Understanding the Decision to Participate in a Survey." *Public Opinion Quarterly,* 1992, *56* (4), 475–495.

Groves, R. M., and Couper, M. P. "Unit Nonresponse in Demographic Surveys." *Proceedings of the Bureau of the Census Annual Research Conference.* Washington, D.C.: Bureau of the Census, 1993.

Groves, R. M., and Couper, M. P. *Householders and Interviewers: The Anatomy of Pre-Interview Interactions.* Survey Methodology Program Working Paper No. 11. Ann Arbor: Survey Research Center, University of Michigan, 1994.

Groves, R. M., and Couper, M. P. "Theoretical Motivation for Post-Survey Nonresponse Adjustment in Household Surveys." *Journal of Official Statistics,* 1995, *11* (1), 93–106.

Groves, R. M., and Couper, M. P. "Contact-Level Influences on Cooperation in Face-to-face Surveys." *Journal of Official Statistics,* 1996.

Groves, R. M., and Kahn, R. L. *Surveys by Telephone.* San Diego: Academic Press, 1979.

Groves, R. M., Raghunathan, T. E., and Couper, M. P. "Evaluating Statistical Adjustments for Unit Nonresponse in a Survey of the Elderly." Paper presented at the Sixth International Workshop on Household Survey Nonresponse, Helsinki, October 1995.

Hawkins, D. F. "Estimation of Nonresponse Bias." *Sociological Methods and Research*, 1975, *3*, 461–488.

Kalton, G. *Compensating for Missing Survey Data*. Ann Arbor: Institute for Social Research, University of Michigan, 1983.

Kemsley, W.F.F. "Family Expenditure Survey: A Study of Differential Response Based on a Comparison of the 1971 Sample with the Census." *Statistical News*, 1975, *31*, 16–21.

Kemsley, W.F.F. "National Food Survey: A Study of Differential Response Based on a Comparison of the 1971 Sample with the Census." *Statistical News*, 1976, *35*, 18–22.

Lievesley, D. "Unit Non-Response in Interview Surveys." Unpublished paper. London: Social and Community Planning Research, 1988.

Lindström, H. L. *Non-Response Errors in Sample Surveys*. Report No. 16. Örebro: Statistics Sweden, 1986.

Little, R., and Rubin, D. B. *Statistical Analysis with Missing Data*. New York: Wiley, 1987.

Mercer, J. R., and Butler, E. W. "Disengagement of the Aged Population and Response Differentials in Survey Research." *Social Forces*, 1967, *46* (1), 89–96.

Morton-Williams, J. *Interviewer Approaches*. Brookfield, Vt.: Dartmouth, 1993.

Norris, P. "The Labour Force Survey: A Study of Differential Response According to Demographic and Socio-Economic Characteristics." *Statistical News*, 1987, *79*, 20–23.

Oksenberg, L., Coleman, L., and Cannell, C. F. "Interviewers' Voices and Refusal Rates in Telephone Surveys." *Public Opinion Quarterly*, 1986, *50* (1), 97–111.

O'Neil, M. J. "Estimating the Nonresponse Bias Due to Refusals in Telephone Surveys." *Public Opinion Quarterly*, 1979, *43*, 218–232.

Paul, E. C., and Lawes, M. "Characteristics of Respondent and Non-Respondent Households in the Canadian Labour Force Survey." *Survey Methodology*, 1982, *8*,48–85.

Petty, R. E., and Cacioppo, J. T. *Communication and Persuasion: Central and Peripheral Routes to Attitude Change*. New York: Springer-Verlag, 1986.

Redpath, B. "Family Expenditure Survey: A Second Study of Differential Response, Comparing Census Characteristics of FES Respondents and Non-Respondents." *Statistical News*, 1986, *72*, 13–16.

Redpath, B., and Elliot, D. "National Food Survey: A Second Study of Differential Response, Comparing Census Characteristics of NFS Respondents and Non-Respondents; Also a Comparison of NFS and FES Response Bias." *Statistical News*, 1988, *80*, 6–10.

Rubin, D. B. *Multiple Imputation for Nonresponse in Surveys*. New York: Wiley, 1986.

Rucker, R. E. "Urban Crime: Fear of Victimization and Perceptions of Risk." *Free Inquiry in Creative Sociology*, 1990, *18* (2), 151–160.

Smith, T. W. "The Hidden 25 Percent: An Analysis of Nonresponse on the 1980 General Social Survey." *Public Opinion Quarterly*, 1983, *47*, 386–404.

MICK P. COUPER *is an assistant research scientist at the Survey Research Center, University of Michigan, and research assistant professor in the Joint Program in Survey Methodology, College Park, Maryland.*

ROBERT M. GROVES *is a research scientist at the Survey Research Center and professor of sociology at the University of Michigan, and a research professor in the Joint Program in Survey Methodology, College Park, Maryland.*

Application of the Rasch model can improve our evaluation of survey data quality.

Applications of the Rasch Model to Evaluation of Survey Data Quality

Kathy E. Green

Data quality appraisal is crucial to useful interpretation of survey results. Design or sampling flaws resulting in biased, incomplete, or unavailable data confound conclusions and lead to bad decisions. Much work in survey research has centered on maximizing response rates to minimize error due to sampling, but relatively less work has targeted effects of question wording and survey design on response quality. This chapter describes the use of the Rasch model to evaluate survey response quality.

Data of high quality, in terms of accuracy, consistency, and validity, are central to good research and evaluation. If our data do not clearly address the research issue, our survey is pointless. If we have collected information that is so biased, tangential, or incomplete that it gives no grounding to our conclusions, the data provide only confusion and misdirection. It seems, then, imperative to assess the quality of survey data prior to presenting results and decisions based upon them. Why, then, is it not common practice to appraise data quality in survey studies? First, some researchers have little or no background in measurement. They may presume that items can be adequately evaluated from surface features (face validity), that one creates measures by adding raw item responses together, and that good survey design assures high-quality data. They would be wrong for some, if not all, of their survey items. Second, researchers' access to the resources and technologies that enable data quality evaluation was limited until recent years.

Variables Affecting Data Quality

This section provides some examples of the effects of common demographic and item-related variables on data quality. The variables considered are education, age, and gender and the sensitivity, ordering, and wording of survey items.

Education. Level of education correlates positively with response rate (for example, Green, in press). While response quality has been examined less frequently, results also indicate a positive relationship between educational level and item completion (Craig and McCann, 1978; Downs and Kerr, 1986; Ferber, 1966–67). Alwin and Krosnick (1991) found a systematic increase in attitude reliability with higher levels of education. Responses increase and improve as educational level increases to college, but may not change with education beyond the undergraduate level.

Age. As the age of respondents increases over the adult years, survey response rate and quality are thought to fall. Kaldenberg, Koenig, and Becker (1994) found deterioration in both response rate and response quality across the age range from sixty-two to ninety-three-plus. Item completion rates have been found to be higher for younger subjects (Downs and Kerr, 1986; Kaldenberg, Koenig, and Becker, 1994). Reliability has been found to decline for the oldest age group (sixty-six to eighty-three), but the amount of decline is small (Sobell and others, 1989).

Gender. Taylor (1976) found women to be more accurate than men in self-coding of occupational categories. Downs and Kerr (1986) found no gender difference in completion of demographic survey items but a small, statistically significant difference in completion of evaluative items, with males completing more items.

Sensitive Items. Reliability estimates vary by item content, with low estimates of reliability found for sensitive items (for example, drug or alcohol use, criminal behavior, and some health-related behavior). Marquis, Marquis, and Polich (1986) found reliability estimates for sensitive items to range from less than .4 to over .9. While on average they found no evidence of systematic bias in reporting (neither under- nor overreporting), the fluctuation in reliability could result in distorted values if items with low reliability are used in subsequent statistical analyses.

Item Order. Substantial differences in response to an item have been found by some when its placement varies within a survey (Schwarz and Hippler, 1995; Tenvergert, Gillespie, Kingma, and Klasen, 1992), while others have found no differences (Sigelman, 1981). Converse and Presser (1986) conclude that item order produces an effect mainly when item content is clearly related across items or when the response to one item implies the response to another. The item order they recommend is to place general items before specific items.

Item Wording and Ambiguity. Seemingly minor changes in item wording can produce shifts in responses, and the direction is often unpredictable.

(See Clark and Schober, 1992, for a discussion.) Clearly, loaded terms influence responses. Single-item measures are particularly susceptible to wording effects unless the item's meaning is virtually unassailable (for example, gender or age). As Davis and Jowell (1989, p. 6) state: "Questionnaires should ideally be made up of *groups* of questions, each group designed to cover a single dimension. . . . Any single question—however careful the design process has been—may in the end turn out to be fatally flawed. . . . Answers to groups of questions on a single dimension should form a pattern. . . . Individual questions whose answers do not conform to the pattern are . . . suspect."

As the studies cited above show, item misinterpretation by respondents can have profound effects on both simple and sophisticated statistical descriptions. The remainder of this chapter describes a measurement model and its application to multi-item scales, which can facilitate data quality appraisal, identification of suspect responses, and construction of conceptually sound measures.

Introduction to the Rasch Model

The Rasch model is one of several item response theoretic (IRT) models and the first choice among those models if one wishes to have understandable variables that measure singular constructs.[1] While the Rasch model was initially used primarily in development and analyses of large-scale achievement tests, it is seeing increasing use in development of psychosocial measures (for example, Bookstein and Lindsay, 1989; Gable, Ludlow, and Wolf, 1990). Martin, Campanelli, and Fay (1991) used Rasch analyses in the survey context to clarify the concept of "work" held by 2,300 respondents to the Current Population Survey. Further possibilities for Rasch model utilization are provided by the availability of software that can now accommodate dichotomous, polytomous, rating scale, and some frequency count data, with application to measurement of latent attitudes as well as latent abilities.

The Rasch model (Rasch, 1960/1980; Wright, 1968) relates a person's "amount" of a trait, attitude, or ability to the probability of her response to an item via specification of a mathematical model. One important benefit of the model is that it can provide estimates of item difficulty or agreeability (item "logits") and person ability or attitude (person "logits") that are relatively invariant over different samples. This invariance is a major advantage in that it moves our deliberations about a measure beyond the particular idiosyncratic data set we derive the measure from. When I measure a person's height, which yardstick I use should be irrelevant, and so it should be with survey measures. This objectivity is obtained with the Rasch model because item logits can be estimated independently of person measures and vice versa.

The quality of any algebraic model's use rests on whether the data meet the model's specifications. The Rasch model's specifications are (1) the set of items measures a single latent construct (the property of unidimensionality). In actuality, unidimensionality is always a fiction, since items and persons are multifaceted. Yet to be useful, measures need to be thought of and behave as though they are reasonably unidimensional. (2) A person's answer to one item is independent of his answers to other items, *except* for the influence of the latent trait (the property of local independence). Items that influence responses to subsequent items—thereby producing item order effect—*violate* this second specification and yield ambiguous calibrations.

Descriptions of the Rasch model have most often employed dichotomous achievement items and have classified responses as being correct (1) or incorrect (0). In this discussion, however, since I am focusing largely on attitude data, I consider the response possibilities to be *degrees of agreement.* Figure 6.1 displays two *item characteristic curves* and shows the relationship between two people's status on the latent trait (their logits) and their likelihood of a positive response to an item. The equation that describes this relationship is:

$$P_i(B) = \frac{e^{B-D}}{1 + e^{B-D}}$$

where $P_i(B)$ is the likelihood of a positive response, B is the logit measure of person attitude, D is the logit measure of item agreeability, and e is the exponential function. As favorability of a person's attitude increases, her or his logit increases, and thus the likelihood of a favorable response increases as well. In Figure 6.1, person B has a higher likelihood of a favorable response to both items 1 and 2 than person A does. Item 2 is harder for both persons A and B to agree with than is item 1. The likelihood of any particular response, then, is determined jointly by the person's attitude and how easy the item is to answer or to agree with. For example, when a person with a strongly favorable attitude answers an item that is easy to agree with, the probability of a strongly favorable response is high. Nothing else is modeled to affect the outcome of the encounter between person and item but her attitude and the item's agreeability. Thus, no accommodation is made for guessing or for interaction of the person with item format or content.

With the Rasch model, answers to individual items are used to estimate person attitude and item position or item agreeability. Raw scores are sufficient statistics for initial estimation of person attitude and item position. When we are estimating a person's attitude, a starting value, such as the logit of his raw score, is used to represent his attitude. Then the probability of observing his particular string of responses is estimated by maximum likelihood. The starting value is improved accordingly and the probability of the string of responses is recalculated. This iterative process continues until the change in the estimates of attitude becomes negligible. This provides estimates for persons and items that maximize the fit of the data to the model.

How well the data fit the model can be evaluated by subtracting expected from observed responses and squaring the result, just the way a chi-square is calculated. These approximately mean square distributed fit statistics are converted to approximate *t*s for ease of interpretation. Once person and item log-

Figure 6.1. Item Characteristic Curves

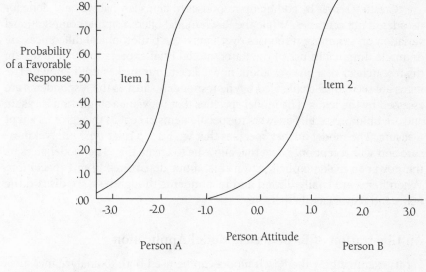

Person A   Person B

its are estimated, the discrepancy between expected and observed values can be calculated for every person-item entry in a data matrix. Discrepancies are typically summed over persons to yield item fit values, and over items to yield person fit values. Determining the fit of the data to the model is conceptually similar to the process used in log-linear or logit analysis, or any analysis that produces expected cell values.

Fit indices tell us, *at the level of the response of an individual person to an individual item* and over a person's total pattern of responses, whether responses are as expected or are suspicious. Fit indices available at the item and person level indicate whether an item fits well with the measure; person fit indices indicate whether a person's responses are so unusual that we question her sincerity. Fit values allow identification of ill-functioning items, suspicious persons, and surprising item-person combinations, and also of responses that fit too well. An item that fits too well may have a socially desirable answer that makes the response to that item redundant.

Other statistics provided with Rasch analysis have counterparts in traditional test theory. First, item discrimination is provided with the point biserial or Pearson correlation coefficient. Second, the index analogous to the KR-20 or Cronbach's alpha is called reliability of person separation. Person separation is the ratio of standard deviation adjusted for measurement error to the root mean square standard error for the sample. It is the number of categories of persons among which the items clearly discriminate.

Finally, the standard error of measurement in traditional test theory takes the same value regardless of person raw score or item position and often misrepresents measurement quality. With the Rasch model, error values are provided for *each* item and person, giving us specific information about measurement quality for persons/items at different points on our "trait ruler."

Creating scores by adding up responses to items is what we have done for decades, if not centuries. While the Rasch model offers a simple computational variation on summing responses over items, the philosophical differences are dramatic. Implicit in use of the Rasch model is an expectation that items are the researcher's best guesses about how a latent trait makes itself known. The items are seen to be challenged by the respondents just as the respondents are assessed by the items. The model specifies that we want a single trait measure and are unimpressed by answers to specific items except as they give us a trait measure. The model further specifies that we want a ruler-type interval measure and will accept only data that allow us to create this. The model gives us the power to make explicit statements about departures from expectation. When items are fatally flawed and respondents thoughtless, we discard the items and reevaluate the persons.

An Illustration of Basic Rasch Model Application

Let us examine how the Rasch model can be used both to analyze measures and to review the patterns of individual respondents.

Measure Analysis. With the Rasch model, the processes of understanding constructs and detecting inadequacies in scales are enhanced by identifying the location of items on an interval scale. Figure 6.2 displays items taken from a mail survey of 154 doctoral graduates and 111 students regarding aspects of completing a dissertation (Green, 1995). The survey included questions about academic background and demographics along with three scales, one of which, the responsibility scale, is discussed here.

The responsibility scale has sixteen items that represent tasks necessary for dissertation completion. For example, item 2 is: "Responsibility for scheduling student-advisor meetings rests with . . . ," and the student supplies a locus of responsibility answer based on a seven-point scale ranging from "student responsibility" (1) to "university/doctoral committee responsibility" (7). Survey data were analyzed using BIGSTEPS (Linacre and Wright, 1991–1994). As illustrated in Figure 6.2, items and persons are presented on the same scale, with higher positive logits indicating perception of greater university as opposed to student responsibility. The construct underlying the set of items is the level of university help needed by students to complete the dissertation. Respondents in this survey perceived themselves to be more responsible for concrete tasks and less responsible for more evaluative tasks. Respondents were not well targeted by the item set as demonstrated by the small overlap between the distribution of persons and the distribution of items. Scale gaps with no items could be filled by asking more questions pertaining to tasks likely to be

Figure 6.2. Responsibility Scale Item-Person Map and Sample Diagnostic Patterns for Two Individual Respondents

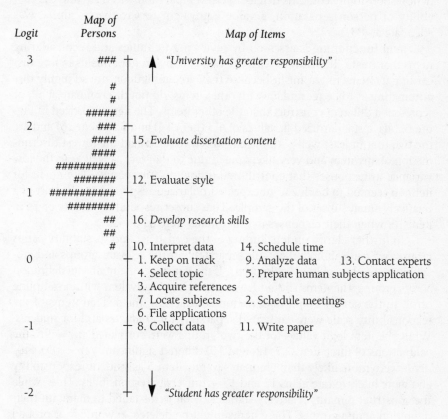

Item-Person Map for Responsibility Scale

Logit	Map of Persons	Map of Items
3	###	↑ *"University has greater responsibility"*
	#	
	#	
	#####	
2	###	
	####	15. *Evaluate dissertation content*
	####	
	##########	
	#######	12. Evaluate style
1	###########	
	########	
	##	16. *Develop research skills*
	##	
	#	10. Interpret data 14. Schedule time
0		1. Keep on track 9. Analyze data 13. Contact experts
		4. Select topic 5. Prepare human subjects application
		3. Acquire references
		7. Locate subjects 2. Schedule meetings
		6. File applications
-1		8. Collect data 11. Write paper
-2		↓ *"Student has greater responsibility"*

Diagnostic Patterns for Two Misfitting Respondents to Responsibility Scale

Respondent 1:   Graduate, Female, Logit 1.20, Fit 4.5, Std. Error .24

Item

	1	2	3	4	5	6	7	8	9	10	11	12	13	14	15	16
RESPONSES: Item 1–16	1	1	1	1	1	1	1	1	7	7	1	1	1	1	7	1
RESIDUALS: Item 1–16									5	4						

Respondent 2:   Graduate, Female, Logit 1.09, Fit 2.8, Std. Error .23

Item

	1	2	3	4	5	6	7	8	9	10	11	12	13	14	15	16
RESPONSES: Item 1–16	1	1	1	1	7	1	1	1	1	1	1	1	7	1	3	7	1
RESIDUALS: Item 1–16					4											

seen as the university's obligation. Moreover, the items did not cover the full range of perceived responsibility. Therefore, items that reflect university responsibility should be added to the measure, and some items reflecting student responsibility could be deleted. Person separation was 2.27, and the reliability of person separation, a value equivalent to Cronbach's alpha, was adequate at .84.

Item functioning is assessed by reviewing fit values and reconsidering items that misfit. It is always wise to evaluate why an item misfits before discarding it. Items might misfit because they are ambiguous, are so highly discriminating as to be redundant with other items, do not discriminate at all, or represent a different construct than the other items. The items italicized in Figure 6.2 have standardized fit values of 4.3 (item 15) and 3.3 (item 16) and are the two that fit least well with the construct. Item 15 had the lowest discrimination of any item and very likely misfit due to that fact as well as to the low variance in responses that contributed to low discrimination. The misfit for item 16 seemed to be due to unexpected polarized responses on the part of a relatively small subset of the sample. That subset responded with 1s or 7s to item 16, when their responses to other items were 3s or 4s.

To further clarify understanding of the construct and its stability *across* groups, we can calibrate the items separately for the relevant groups and create bivariate plots of item calibrations. If the construct maintains its definition across groups, the items should have calibrations equivalent within sampling error. In the survey about dissertation completion, the sixteen items of the responsibility scale were calibrated separately for *graduates* and for *students*. While the item logit values for the two groups were correlated at $r = .96$, the calibrations of three items (5, 12, and 15) differed significantly ($p < .05$). Students were more likely than graduates to rate item 5 as student responsibility and more likely to rate items 12 and 15 as university responsibility. Thus, while the construct remains relatively stable, several items failed to maintain their definition across groups. These items might be deleted, reworded, or probed for their differential meaning by consulting with a group of students and graduates. Item 15 both misfit *and* was understood differently by students and graduates, and this item might be simply deleted to clarify the scale.

Person Response Review. After items have been reviewed and the analysis rerun (if items are discarded), we proceed to examine person fit, a value aggregated across the items that a person answered. Person responses may misfit because the individual lied, cheated, did not take the task seriously, ran out of time, misread items, did not understand items, acted on a response set (such as extreme responding), or changed his view midway through the questions. The computer program provides fit values and item residuals for each item-person combination. These clues can be used to generate hypotheses about a person's behavior. We can combine our information about person fit with knowledge of demographic or other characteristics to see whether, for example, different age groups' responses fit better or worse. As another example, person fit values in a drug use survey of adolescents could be used to identify teenagers who may be deceptive. Note, however, that if a person provides inaccurate but consistent responses, the inaccuracy will not be detected.

Of the persons responding to the doctoral dissertation survey, thirteen misfit (standardized fit > 2.0) by giving unexpected responses to some items; further, eighteen persons' data fit too well, that is, these respondents had so little deviation from expectation that one might wonder if they were honest or were providing socially conforming views (standardized fit < -2.0). These people's standardized mean square residual was over two standard deviations away from the expected value of 0.0. The thirteen persons with unexpected responses were more often graduates (ten out of the thirteen) than students and gave highly unexpected responses to one or two items rather than somewhat unexpected responses to numerous items. In the example shown in Figure 6.2, respondent 1 felt that responsibility for analyzing and interpreting data rests with the university, not the student (residuals of 5 and 4); respondent 2 felt the university, not the student, should arrange for filing the application for human subjects review (residual of 4). Misfitting patterns displayed no random responding or discernible misunderstanding of questions but seemed rather to evoke responses to sore points for the graduates. People whose response patterns fit too well may have nonattitudes or ambivalent opinions about the subject.

An error value is generated for each item and person in the data matrix (in contrast to a single error value generated in traditional test theory). Figure 6.2, for example, shows values of .24 and .23 as the standard errors for the two sample respondents. If one wished to increase the precision of measurement for individuals, providing more items close to the respondent's attitude logit would accomplish this. If one wished to know whether some subgroups, such as graduates or students, are measured more accurately than others, the fit values and standard errors for subgroups could be compared.

The Rasch Model and Survey Data

The following section summarizes how application of the Rasch model can aid data quality appraisal and survey research efficiency.

When several items address the same construct, responses to the items can be aggregated to form a more reliable summary scale. With the Rasch model, a summary measure can be estimated that has two notable advantages over traditional methods: the measure is interval in structure and the extent to which the data fit the model is assessed. This contrasts with scales formed under traditional test theory, which are ordinal and have no test of whether the data fit the model. When responses to items are given on multipoint rating scales, the steps of the scale will be converted to interval distances as well. The Rasch model places items and persons on a common scale so we can visualize the utility of the items for the sample by seeing how well the items are targeted on the persons. Items are located as points on the scale. If we understand why the items are ordered and spaced as they are, and can compose items and know approximately where they will fit on the trait ruler, we have come a long way toward truly understanding the construct measured. Validity is addressed directly by Rasch model application via construct understanding. We can also calibrate items separately for subgroups and examine whether the construct's definition remains stable across subgroups. If not, we had best review our items with members of the subgroups to evaluate their meaning.

The item calibrations derived from Rasch model analysis are called *sample free,* because their values are independent of the distribution of person scores. This does not mean we can obtain descriptions of persons or items without data nor does it mean we can ask the wrong people irrelevant questions. It does mean that the measures of persons are algebraically freed from the calibrations of items. We can ask different groups of people different questions and, as long as some core of items or persons links all the data together, derive commensurate estimates for items and persons across different survey forms and also over time. If a survey is very long and imposes a high burden on respondents, not everyone needs to answer all of the items. The survey can be segmented, with systematic portions of each measure given to different random subsamples. The idea is similar to multiple matrix sampling (Shoemaker, 1973).

The ability to characterize subgroups whose response patterns fit differentially is useful in the following ways. First, it is of practical value to survey designers to know whether data from, say, an Asian American group fit better or worse than data from a Hispanic or Anglo group. We can redesign surveys to be targeted on subgroups, with different types of items, different numbers of items, and different wording in instructions to adjust for fit differences. Fit can be a variable used in subsequent analyses. Second, on a theoretical level, knowledge of differential fit associated with subgroup characteristics allows us to explore ideas about group behaviors and cognitions. Third, removal of persons with misfitting responses from a data set opens the door to clearer discernment of patterns among variables. Less noise enhances signal detection. The criterion for removing cases from a data set rests on the researcher's judgment, just as identification of outliers would. Examination of and possible removal of cases with fit values over +2.0 would generally be reasonable.

A recent development in Rasch models, *facets analysis* (Linacre and Wright, 1989–1994), enables us to evaluate the effects on responses of demographic or manipulated variables such as ethnicity, gender, wording variations, item placement, and other specific item characteristics. While effects of these factors are not remediated by use of Rasch model techniques, we are afforded information about their extent and are guided to future revision accommodating this knowledge.

Researchers should note that the Rasch model is a scaling model, used to construct measures from multiple observations, and so its applicability to the evaluation of single-item indicators is limited. On rare occasions, a diverse set of loosely related items can be combined to create a measure, and thus misfitting items and suspicious person responses can be identified, but more often the model will not be relevant for analysis of single items.

For more detailed treatments of Rasch model applications, the reader is referred to Wright and Masters (1982) and Linacre and Wright (1989–1994).

Conclusion

This chapter began with a review of effects of selected factors on the quality of survey data. Data quality can vary widely across item sets and samples, and we need to be aware of measurement error as well as sampling error in our data. Rasch model programs yield rich information about items, persons, and subgroup responses. While originally applied in the United Stated with large-scale achievement testing, Rasch analysis is of value in small- to medium-scale efforts as well. It sees applications in identifying the underlying dimension of meaning that accounts for individuals' responses, in designing and refining scales, in identifying problems in respondent comprehension of items, in identifying the failure of some items to contribute to definition of the variable, in finding whether measures remain stable across population subgroups, in estimating parameters from incomplete data, and in objectively comparing values over different populations and time periods. The stringent requirements and widespread applicability of the Rasch model yield strong measures of many of the constructs used in survey research.

Note

1. The Rasch model is a one-parameter IRT model. More general two- and three-parameter models exist that may provide better fit to data, but these more general IRT models have problems in that (1) parameters may not be estimable and (2) the resulting measures are blends of multiple constructs and so violate principles of *fundamental* measurement (Krantz, Luce, Suppes, and Tversky, 1971).

References

Alwin, D. F., and Krosnick, J. A. "The Reliability of Survey Attitude Measurement." *Sociological Methods & Research,* 1991, *20,* 139–181.

Bookstein, A., and Lindsay, A. "Questionnaire Ambiguity: A Rasch Scaling Model Analysis." *Library Trends,* 1989, *38,* 215–236.

Clark, H. H., and Schober, M. F. "Asking Questions and Influencing Answers." In J. M. Tanur (ed.), *Questions About Questions: Inquiries into the Cognitive Bases of Surveys.* New York: Russell Sage, 1992.

Converse, J. M., and Presser, S. *Survey Questions.* Newbury Park, Calif.: Sage, 1986.

Craig, C. S., and McCann, J. M. "Item Nonresponse in Mail Surveys: Extent and Correlates." *Journal of Marketing Research,* 1978, *15,* 285–289.

Davis, J. A., and Jowell, R. "Measuring National Differences: An Introduction to the International Social Survey Programme (ISSP)." In Jowell, R. (ed.), *British Social Attitudes: Special International Report.* London: Gower, 1989.

Downs, P. E., and Kerr, J. R. "Recent Evidence on the Relationship Between Anonymity and Response Variables for Mail Surveys." *Journal of the Academy of Marketing Science,* 1986, *14,* 72–82.

Ferber, R. "Item Nonresponse in a Consumer Survey." *Public Opinion Quarterly,* 1966–67, *30,* 399–415.

Gable, R. K., Ludlow, L. H., and Wolf, M. B. "The Use of Classical and Rasch Latent Trait Models to Enhance the Validity of Affective Measures." *Educational and Psychological Measurement,* 1990, *50,* 869–878.

Green, K. E. *Academic Procrastination and Perfectionism: A Comparison of Graduates and ABDs.* Paper presented at the annual meeting of the American Educational Research Association, San Francisco, Apr. 1995.

Green, K. E. "Sociodemographic Factors and Mail Survey Response." *Psychology and Marketing,* in press.

Kaldenberg, D. O., Koenig, H. F., and Becker, B. W. "Mail Survey Response Rate Patterns in a Population of the Elderly: Does Response Deteriorate with Age?" *Public Opinion Quarterly,* 1994, *58,* 68–76.

Krantz, D. H., Luce, R. D., Suppes, P., and Tversky, A. *Foundations of Measurement: Additive and Polynomial Representations.* Vol. 1. San Diego: Academic Press, 1971.

Linacre, J. M., and Wright, B. D. *FACETS.* Chicago: MESA Press, 1989–1994.

Linacre, J. M., and Wright, B. D. *A User's Guide to BIGSTEPS.* Chicago: MESA Press, 1991–1994.

Marquis, N.T.H., Marquis, M. S., and Polich, J. M. "Response Bias and Reliability in Sensitive Topic Surveys." *Journal of the American Statistical Association,* 1986, *81,* 381–389.

Martin, E. A., Campanelli, P. C., and Fay, R. E. "An Application of Rasch Analysis to Questionnaire Design: Using Vignettes to Study the Meaning of 'Work' in the Current Population Survey." *The Statistician,* 1991, *40,* 265–276.

Rasch, G. *Probabilistic Models for Some Intelligence and Attainment Tests.* Copenhagen: Danmarke Paedagogiske Institut, 1960. (Expanded edition, Chicago: MESA Press, 1980.)

Schwarz, N., and Hippler, H. J. "Reverse Context Effects in Mail Surveys." *Public Opinion Quarterly,* 1995, *59,* 93–97.

Shoemaker, D. M. *Principles and Procedures of Multiple Matrix Sampling.* Cambridge, Mass.: Ballinger, 1973.

Sigelman, L. "Question-Order Effects on Presidential Popularity." *Public Opinion Quarterly,* 1981, *45,* 199–207.

Sobell, J., Block, G., Koslowe, P., Tobin, J., and Andres, R. "Validation of a Retrospective Questionnaire Assessing Diet 10–15 Years Ago." *American Journal of Epidemiology,* 1989, *130,* 173–187.

Taylor, G. "The Accuracy of Respondent-Coded Occupation." *Public Opinion Quarterly,* 1976, *40,* 245–255.

Tenvergert, E., Gillespie, M. W., Kingma, J., and Klasen, H. "Abortion Attitudes, 1984–1987–1988: Effects of Item Order and Dimensionality." *Perceptual and Motor Skills,* 1992, *74,* 627–642.

Wright, B. D. "Sample-Free Test Calibration and Person Measurement." In *Proceedings of the 1967 Invitational Conference on Testing Problems.* Princeton, N.J.: Educational Testing Service , 1968.

Wright, B. D., and Masters, G. N. *Rating Scale Analysis.* Chicago: MESA Press/University of Chicago, 1982.

KATHY E. GREEN is professor of education, University of Denver, Denver, Colorado.

The rapid increase in non-English-speaking populations within the United States dictates the need for well-translated instruments to reduce nonresponse and measurement error in surveys.

Translating Survey Questionnaires: Lessons Learned

Ruth B. McKay, Martha J. Breslow, Roberta L. Sangster, Susan M. Gabbard, Robert W. Reynolds, Jorge M. Nakamoto, John Tarnai

Until recently, the standard translation practice of many survey organizations was to have questionnaires translated into a second language by one or more bilingual persons in the organizations who were knowledgeable about the survey concepts (Marín and Marín, 1991). Pretesting of the translated instruments was not standard practice. Recent postsurvey evaluations of survey instruments produced by this method have identified multiple problems in their construction (Gabbard and Nakamoto, 1994). This chapter discusses factors that help make a translated instrument more comparable to the original survey instrument as well as more comprehensible to the respondent. Three case studies illustrate issues associated with the translation process.

Translation Methods and Objectives

Translators typically use either of two main methods of translation: direct (one-way) translation or back-translation. In direct translation, a bilingual person translates the source (original) language instrument into the target (second) language. A variation of this method is "translation by committee," in which two or more bilingual individuals independently translate the source instrument into the target language and then compare and reconcile their translations.

This chapter grew out of a session presented at an American Association for Public Opinion Research meeting in Danvers, Massachusetts, in May 1994.

Back-translation is more complex. As described by Bernard (1988), it entails three stages. First, the instrument is translated from the source language into the target language by a bilingual translator. Second, another bilingual translator translates the target instrument back into the source language. Finally, the original and back-translated versions are compared and the target language instrument is modified until it accurately reflects the source language instrument. While back-translation is considered the method of choice by many, proponents of this method acknowledge that because the first translator may strive to keep the grammatical constructions of the source language in order to arrive at an identical second version in the source language, there is a danger that the target language instrument may be stilted, awkwardly worded, or even incomprehensible (Marín and Marín, 1991).

If modification of the source language instrument is acceptable, a strategy called *decentering* may be used with either translation method to produce survey instruments that are conceptually equivalent across languages (Werner and Campbell, 1970). In decentering, the instrument written in the source language is not considered final until the entire translation process has been completed. As the translation or back-translation process reveals words or phrases in the source language that are problematic in the target language, revisions are made in both the source and target language instruments until comparable questions are achieved in both languages.

Ideally, whatever the translation method chosen, it will be used to achieve an explicitly stated translation objective: literal translation, conceptual translation, or culturally equivalent translation. In *literal translation,* the translator uses terms or phrases in the target language that are the dictionary equivalents of the terms in the source language instrument. *Conceptual translation* uses terms or phrases in the target language that capture the implied associations, or connotative meaning, of the text used in the source language instrument. *Culturally equivalent translation* extends the conceptual equivalence of words and phrases in the source instrument to tap equivalent patterns of thought and behavior in the social world of the target language speakers. It is important that the objective of the translation be explicitly identified before translators begin their work.

Postsurvey Evaluations of Translated Instruments

On occasion, postsurvey evaluations will identify problems with translated instruments. For example, two separate postsurvey evaluations of the 1990 Spanish language U.S. Census form found that literal translations of English phrasing led to stilted or actually misleading constructions in the Spanish form (Elias-Olivares and Farr, 1991; Kissam, Herrera, and Nakamoto, 1993). As a result, the Spanish vocabulary in the Census form was found to be too technical or formal and to use unfamiliar terms. Comprehension of the Spanish translation required a respondent reading level higher than that required for the English version. Low-literacy respondents found many of the common conventions used in survey forms—such as parenthetical instructions and instructions for skip patterns—difficult to understand, and this contributed to the respondents' perception that completing the Census form was extremely burdensome (Kissam, Herrera, and Nakamoto, 1993). Respondents also considered separate questions on race, Hispanic origin, and ethnicity to be redundant, because the three terms draw on a single undifferentiated concept for the majority of Hispanics. Furthermore, the cultural background of many Hispanic respondents provided no frame of reference for interpreting such concepts as "confidentiality," "household," and "year of entry."

The Growing Body of Translation Theory and Practice

In the last decade, sociolinguistics, ethnography, cognitive psychology, and survey research methodology have contributed to a new and growing body of survey translation theory and practice (McKay and Lavallee, 1993). Sociolinguistics has increased our understanding of how literal and conceptual translation result in very different products. Literal translation does not take into account that a target language will exhibit significant linguistic variation depending upon the speaker's national origin (such as Mexico versus Argentina) and regional location within the United States. Nor does literal translation take into account the fluid, evolving nature of language. For example, sociohistorical circumstances lead immigrants to create languages rich in loan words drawn from their new culture. Elias-Olivares and Farr (1991) observed that Spanish monolinguals—people who know only Spanish—involved in new experiences in the United States such as buying a house quite naturally borrow words from English, such as "las taxas" (los impuestos) and "real estate" (bienes raices), in order to fill gaps in their native language. Although equivalents of the English terms exist in standard Spanish, they were not part of the immigrants' vocabulary because they were not part of the immigrants' experience until they came to the United States.

The field of ethnography has also contributed new approaches to developing multilingual surveys. Ethnography views phenomena from an emic perspective (that is, as occurring within the culturally patterned worldview shared by members of a particular community or society) and cautions against assuming that the values and behavior patterns of mainstream society are universally shared. Ethnographic methodology, especially participant observation, has provided a set of tools for pretesting translated questionnaires. Drawing from this field, McKay (1993) observed households in a Salvadoran community prior to pretesting the Spanish version of the Redesigned Current Population Survey.

The "cognitive aspects of survey methodology" movement also offers observational techniques for pretesting and evaluating survey instruments. These include concurrent and retrospective "think aloud" interviews, respondent and interviewer debriefing procedures, and behavior coding of monitored interviews (Royston, Bercini, Sirken, and Mingay, 1986).

Against this background, we now present three case studies that address such issues as selecting a translation method, identifying the translation objectives, securing and training competent translators, managing the translation process, pretesting translated instruments, and training interviewers. The case studies also describe approaches to resolving problems inherent in the survey translation process.

Case study 1 describes how the direct translation method was used to achieve a conceptual translation in Spanish. Case study 2, involving two survey instruments, illustrates the use of the back-translation method to develop a literal translation for the first survey instrument. Then, because of lessons learned during that task, direct translation with decentering was used to develop a conceptual translation for the second survey instrument. Case study 3 describes how the back-translation model was used to achieve literal translations in six target languages.

Case Study 1: 1992 Health and Retirement Study

The 1992 Health and Retirement Study (HRS) was a panel study of U.S. residents born between 1931 and 1941. The survey's purpose was to gain a better understanding of the factors that affect an individual's decision to retire from the paid labor force and the subsequent consequences of retirement on health and economic well-being. Most of the survey questions sought factual information about health, work, family structure, and finances. The sample was nationally representative and included a 1.7 oversample of Hispanics, primarily Mexican Americans. Interviews were conducted either face-to-face or by telephone.

Translation Process. The goal of the translation was to produce a conceptual translation into Spanish using a direct translation process. A major concern was to address national or regional differences in Spanish as it is spoken and understood in the United States. Words and phrases commonly used by one group may be incomprehensible, or sometimes offensive, to another group. Another concern was that many of the Spanish-speaking respondents would have limited education. In some cases, they might not be familiar with standard dictionary terminology.

The translation team consisted of a lead translator, edit translators, and a staff coordinator. The lead translator was selected to be of the same ethnic background (Mexican American) as the majority of Spanish-speaking respondents. The edit translators were from different Hispanic national backgrounds, thus bringing varied linguistic and cultural perspectives to the translation. All group members participated in a training session to ensure that they understood the objectives of the translation, the translation process, and the time schedule for the project.

The lead translator prepared the initial translation. The edit translators and the coordinator then read the translation and compared it to the English instrument, noting errors, poor phrasing, words that might not be understood by all national groups, and other problems. The entire group then met to discuss and resolve the discrepancies between the target and source instruments and to revise the target instrument accordingly. The discrepancies between the source instrument and the initial translation were generally quite subtle (for example, choice of a synonym that had a different connotative meaning from the English term) and were often identified by the coordinator rather than the translators because they were not as familiar as the coordinator with the question objectives.

Once an acceptable translation was achieved, it was sent to a Spanish-speaking field supervisor and an interviewer for review. Their experience in interviewing Spanish speakers in the Southwest United States was expected to provide the best sense of what respondents in that region would understand. After revising the instrument once more, it was formally pretested with Spanish-speaking respondents who had a variety of national backgrounds and who met the study's eligibility criteria. The interviewers, translators, and coordinator then held a debriefing to evaluate the results of the pretest and resolve remaining problems in the Spanish survey instrument.

Finally, interviewers were thoroughly trained on the English questionnaire before being trained on the Spanish version. New interviewers received face-to-face training on translation objectives and special conventions, while interviewers already in the field were mailed the translated questionnaire and a cover memo containing survey instructions.

Lessons Learned. An understanding of the national, regional, and educational characteristics of the target language population, together with the goal of producing a conceptual translation, influenced the recruitment and training of translators, the decision to use a group approach in the translation process, and the methods of pretesting the translated survey instrument.

Translators' and interviewers' understanding of the survey objectives will be enhanced through initial training on the English instrument. In this case study, even though the coordinator met with the translators to agree upon the objectives, procedures, and schedule, a dispute arising in the first group working meeting made it apparent that the translation objectives had not been adequately discussed. Thorough training of translators and interviewers is important because question meaning is often not as self-evident as we may think; subtle differences in meaning across different language versions can easily affect response distributions. Finally, input from others besides the translators, such as the interviewers and pretest respondents, is useful in gauging the target community's ability to understand and respond to the questions as translated.

Case Study 2: Spanish Redesigned Current Population Survey and Spanish CPS Supplement on Race and Ethnicity

The Current Population Survey (CPS) is a joint Bureau of Labor Statistics (BLS) and Census monthly labor force survey of 60,000 households, conducted by personal and telephone interview. This case study describes the development of two survey instruments: the Spanish translation of the redesigned CPS and the Spanish version CPS Supplement on Race and Ethnicity.

Instrument 1: Current Population Survey. The national CPS sample includes approximately 3,000 Hispanic households. When the CPS questionnaire was redesigned in the early 1990s, a Spanish version of the questionnaire was developed. There were no formal objectives stated at the start of that translation process (regarding conceptual versus literal translation, for example) other than the goal of producing a Spanish-language instrument that would be equally well understood by members of the major Hispanic national origin groups (for example, Mexican, Puerto Rican, and Cuban). Bernard's (1988) back-translation model was used, with input from translators representing the major national origin groups.

Translation Process. The source instrument was first translated into Spanish by a bilingual Census staff member of Cuban origin with training in literary translation. Next, bilingual Hispanic economists from Cuba, El Salvador, Puerto Rico, Bolivia, and Mexico independently back-translated the target questionnaire into English. The lead translator and the back-translators met to negotiate the best vocabulary choices across the national origin groups. In those few cases in which no single Spanish term could express a survey term across all Hispanic groups, two Spanish terms separated by a slash were used, with interviewer instructions to use the term appropriate for the national background of the respondent. In addition, words or phrases that were awkward or stilted in the Spanish version by virtue of being literal translations of the English were modified to more natural Spanish constructions. For example, *mensualmente,* the literal Spanish term for "monthly," is a word which few Spanish speakers would use; it was replaced by *por mes* ("by month"), which Spanish speakers of all educational levels would use.

The Spanish instrument was next sent to bilingual Hispanic CPS interviewers in New York, Los Angeles, Dallas, and Miami. These interviewers participated in a teleconference to discuss regional differences in Spanish language use and to negotiate the best words or phrases to be used in the questionnaire. As before, in instances where more than one Spanish term was required, two terms separated by a slash were used (for example, *sindicato/union*). A total of seven double terms were required in the final Spanish instrument. The interviewers' concerns about the questionnaire's level of difficulty led to twenty additional changes in vocabulary or phrasing to make the questionnaire intelligible to respondents with little formal education.

A modified form of cognitive interview using the Spanish questionnaire was conducted with paid respondents of Mexican origin in rural and urban California locations. Respondents with less than a high school education were recruited for this pilot test because fewer than 50 percent of Mexican Americans over the age of twenty-five have completed high school (Cattan, 1993) and approximately 65 percent of Hispanic CPS respondents are of Mexican origin. Standard cognitive interview procedure calls for the participant to "think aloud" when answering a question or to paraphrase the question after answering it. In the pretest of the Spanish CPS, the researcher first observed computer-assisted interviews conducted by Spanish-speaking CPS interviewers. Following the formal interview, the researcher spoke with each respondent about questions that appeared to have been difficult to comprehend or otherwise problematic.

The cognitive interviews revealed that this population had problems in responding because of the very formal language constructions used in the questions and a lack of familiarity with some of the vocabulary. Attempts to resolve these problems brought to light previously unrecognized differences among the translation project team members in their assumptions about the objectives of the translation and, to a lesser extent, the national groups' differences in linguistic traditions. As an example, the lead translator and the back-translation team had decided that the word *inquilino* was the best Spanish term for "boarder." When the cognitive research on the questionnaire was carried out with respondents of Mexican origin, none reported having boarders in their households. However, during the discussions following the interviews, several respondents revealed that they did indeed have boarders, whom they termed *renteros*. None of the respondents were familiar with the term *inquilino*. When it was suggested that *rentero* be included alongside *inquilino,* however, the lead translator and the back-translation team protested. Even though the dictionary defines *rentero* as a taxpayer or rural tenant, the term was not considered by the translators to be proper Spanish. Notwithstanding the fact that respondents of Mexican origin with less than a high school education constitute the largest single group within the Hispanic CPS sample, the translators insisted that the CPS, as an official U.S. government survey, should not use a level of language that "would reflect badly" on the government. In this case, the translators prevailed and the word *rentero* was not used.

Lessons Learned. The lessons made apparent by this experience are discussed below, together with the lessons learned from the translation of the CPS supplement.

Instrument 2: Spanish Language CPS Supplement on Race and Ethnicity. The CPS Supplement on Race and Ethnicity was designed to test alternative forms of questions on race, ethnicity, and ancestry for the year 2000 Census. The protocol developed for the Spanish translation of the supplement attempted to avoid the problems of stilted phrasing and obscure vocabulary resulting from back-translation. Instead, direct translation with decentering was used.

Translation Process. The translation was carried out independently by professional translators of Mexican, Cuban, and Puerto Rican origin. The objective of the translation was to produce a questionnaire that would be intelligible to Hispanics across a wide range of educational levels, national origins, geographical regions, and length of residence within the United States. Following completion of the three independent Spanish translations, differences were reconciled in a two-hour teleconference. The questionnaire resulting from the reconciliation conference was reviewed by a bilingual BLS Hispanic economist with translation training.

Cognitive research on both the English and Spanish versions was carried out concurrently to allow for decentering of problematic terms encountered in either instrument. Cognitive interviews using the Spanish questionnaire were conducted with Hispanics in New York, Washington, D.C., Houston, and rural and urban California. The interviews revealed that, with one exception, the same problems were surfacing in both the English and Spanish instruments and were due to the difficulty of the survey questions. Parallel revisions to the source and target language questionnaires resulted in a final instrument that proved to be readily understandable in both languages. The one exception concerned the Spanish translation of the English question, "Which group do you identify with?" This was understood by Hispanics as, "Which group do you get along with?" Decentering led to a rewording of the question in both languages as, "Which group do you belong to?"

Lessons Learned. In the Spanish translation of the CPS, the use of translators representing the major Hispanic national origin groups and the strategy of providing several alternative translations for certain terms avoided misunderstanding of questions by Hispanic respondents of certain national origins. However, the lack of initial discussion and agreement about the objective of producing a questionnaire that would be understandable across educational levels led to a very formal literal translation of the source questionnaire. Strict adherence to the back-translation model produced a Spanish instrument with a number of convoluted questions. In some cases, elitism on the part of the translators discouraged the inclusion of less formal terms that would be more familiar to respondents.

The translation of the supplement attempted to avoid the pitfalls encountered during the translation of the redesigned CPS. Translators were recruited and trained to produce a conceptual rather than a formal literal translation of the source instrument. In addition, because the source language instrument was not finalized at the time of the translation, it was possible to use a decentering strategy to make revisions in both the source and target language instruments. The decentering strategy worked well, and the supplement met its objective of being comprehensible to Hispanics from a wide range of backgrounds.

Case Study 3: Washington State
Substance Abuse Prevalence Project Survey

This case study describes a statewide study of alcohol and drug prevalence conducted by the Social and Economics Sciences Research Center (SESRC) in Pullman, Washington. The research procedures involved translating the lengthy survey instrument into the six primary languages, other than English, that are spoken in Washington State: Cambodian (Khmer), Vietnamese, Korean, Cantonese, Japanese, and Spanish. Once operational, the study would average 500 telephone interviews with statewide residents each month over a one-year period (1993 to 1994).

The survey instrument consisted of fifteen sections with very complicated skip patterns. The sections covered sensitive topics including alcohol and drug use and abuse, treatment history, and diagnosis and treatment of mental disorders. The source language questions were often technical, and many used U.S. slang to describe drug and alcohol use. While some sections were asked of all respondents, others began with screening questions designed to skip respondents out of inapplicable sections. At other points, a computer program summed responses from prior sections to determine the respondent's eligibility for the next section.

The translation objective was to achieve literal translations in the six languages to match the English (source) instrument as nearly as possible. A back-translation model was used for the translation process (Bernard, 1988). It was later determined that literal translation proved to be less than adequate to meet the demands of this complex survey.

Translation Process. The first task was to recruit native speakers of the six target languages who were also fluent in English. Identifying individuals with these language skills near the project site, in rural Washington State, was particularly challenging. The translators' skills in writing, grammar, and vocabulary usage varied by virtue of such circumstances as whether they had left their home countries as students or refugees, whether they had left recently or many years before, and what their ages were when emigrating. Even for fluent bilinguals, the specialized vocabulary used in the study was difficult to translate and required an ability to conceptualize new ideas and articulate them in the target language.

The translators needed to have an open and flexible perspective on the world. They frequently did not share the researchers' perspectives and knowledge about drug and alcohol abuse or the belief that the survey topic was of importance. They needed to be educated about the project so that the significance of the research would be appropriately communicated to members of the target language groups, because respondents' level of willingness to participate and the quality of their responses can vary according to the legitimacy given the survey topic and its questions.

Translators were instructed on the back-translation method and the objective of developing literal translations of the source language instrument. Discussions of each survey question revealed that nuances of meaning and subject-specific vocabulary, such as "halfway house" or "detox," were the hardest for the translators to comprehend and translate.

Because of differences in the time necessary to translate and back-translate in the different languages, the six translations and the pretesting of the translations were completed at different times, some translations taking several weeks longer than others. Pretesting took place as soon as a translation was completed. The Spanish, Japanese, and Vietnamese translations were completed first. Pretesting and training of interviewers for these three translations occurred simultaneously and in three phases.

The first phase of testing entailed having the interviewers practice reading the questionnaire aloud in an empty room and entering fabricated data into the computer system. The second test of each translated instrument employed telephone calls in which subjects role-played scenarios. Identities with specific characteristics were fabricated in order to test the questions in the fifteen-part survey. The last test of the instrument took place when each interviewer completed two telephone interviews with target language speakers identified during the pretest of the English instrument. Once a translated survey instrument had been pretested, translators used group consensus to revise the target language instrument.

Literal translation proved to be a problem during the pretests. Interviewers found the literal translations difficult to read aloud, which made it difficult for the respondents to understand the questions. The literal translation lacked the flow found in the normal speaking patterns of the languages; the translated text felt and sounded awkward. While the use of target-language dictionaries had proven helpful for the clarification of unfamiliar terms, dictionaries could not be relied upon to produce understandable text.

Because the Spanish, Japanese, and Vietnamese translations were the first to be pretested, it was possible to use their pretest results to improve the survey translations in the remaining three languages. The Cantonese, Cambodian, and Korean translators were asked to maintain the meaning of the question but were also instructed to phrase the question in a normal conversational pattern for the target language and to employ commonly used words rather than dictionary translations. The approach favored in this later phase of the project was to describe to the translator the meaning of the English term with which he or she was unfamiliar, following which the translator would translate that description rather than use the dictionary term. This approach also encouraged translators to discuss any unfamiliar terms with the survey managers. Pretesting of the three instruments that were translated last showed that this approach produced more intelligible translations than those achieved for the earlier Spanish, Japanese, and Vietnamese versions.

Pretesting also revealed that various deferments and formal apologies traditionally used in the target languages when asking personal or sensitive questions were missing from the instruments. These needed to be added to avoid offending respondents, which would have increased refusals. For example, a reference to "you" is not considered polite in Korean conversation, and these references were deleted from the Korean questionnaire. Allowing these changes deviated from Bernard's (1988) translation model but created a more culturally sensitive survey instrument.

Lessons Learned. First, avoid literal translations. While these are grammatically correct and follow the wording of the original text, they may be too formal for the average speaker, convoluting the language to borderline comprehensibility. Next, when creating the source language instrument, avoid the use of slang and technical terms, which may not translate well into other languages. Also keep modifiers and examples to a minimum. Modifiers and examples used to increase comprehension in the source instrument added to the difficulty of translating the instrument. Some examples simply did not translate while others were foreign to the different cultures. The examples also tended to get very long in translation, exacerbating an already existing problem of length. Next, try to use questions, phrases, and examples that are culturally sensitive and that fit the life experiences of the persons to be interviewed. To be sensitive to the linguistic style of the target community, ask the translators to indicate which questions might be offensive or be missing important polite phrases necessary for good form in an interview. Finally, as with any survey instrument, thorough pretesting of all aspects is the best way to discover potential pitfalls in a translated questionnaire.

Conclusion

Conceptual translation as an objective is highly recommended. Even the least resource-intensive translation method, direct (one-way) translation, was effective when conceptual translation was the objective. Case study 1 demonstrated that having a group of people carry out the direct translation method with conceptual translation as the objective worked well when proper attention was given to the range of regional, national origin, and educational characteristics of the target language respondents.

When literal translation was the objective, even the more thorough method, back-translation, did not result in optimal translations in the Current Population Survey and the Washington State Substance Abuse Prevalence Survey. In both cases, when dictionary definitions were used during translation, the integrity of the questions was compromised. These projects demonstrated that identification of conceptual translation as an objective should take place at the onset of the project and that translators who have the skills needed to carry out conceptual translation should be recruited and trained accordingly. Training for conceptual translation should stress the importance of the cultural background of the target language speakers, including the knowledge, beliefs, and values associated with the survey subject matter, and the culturally patterned rules of polite discourse within their community.

Decentering was used effectively in translating the CPS Supplement on Race and Ethnicity. While decentering of source and target language instruments is not often feasible, due to either insufficient time or multiple target languages, consideration should be given to amending the source version if insurmountable problems arise in creating conceptually equivalent questions in the target language.

These three case studies illustrate the complexity of the translation process and the interaction between the choice of method and the translation objective. The success of any translation effort will depend upon a multitude of factors, attention to which should result in both greater validity of the data and higher response rates.

References

Bernard, H. R. *Research Methods in Cultural Anthropology*. Newbury Park, Calif.: Sage, 1988.
Cattan, P. "The Diversity of Hispanics in the U.S. Work Force." *Monthly Labor Review*, 1993, *116* (8), 3–15.

Elias-Olivares, L., and Farr, M. *Sociolinguistic Analysis of Mexican-American Patterns of Non-Response to Census Questionnaires*. Ethnographic Exploratory Research Report No. 16. Washington, D.C.: Bureau of the Census, 1991.

Gabbard, S. M., and Nakamoto, J. "Evaluating Translations of Survey Instruments in Spanish and English: The 1990 Spanish Language Census Long Form." Paper presented at the American Association for Public Opinion Research meeting, Danvers, Mass., May 1994.

Kissam, E., Herrera, E., and Nakamoto, J. M. *Hispanic Response to Census Enumeration: Forms and Procedures*. Report submitted to the Census Bureau, Contract No. 50-YABC-2–66027, Task Order No. 46-YABC-2–0001. Washington D.C.: Bureau of the Census, March 1993.

McKay, R. B. "Undercoverage of Hispanics in Household Surveys." *Monthly Labor Review*, 1993, *116* (9), 38–42.

McKay, R. B., and Lavallee, A. P. "The Hispanic Version of the Redesigned CPS Questionnaire: Applying Sociolinguistic and Survey Research Methods to Translating Survey Questionnaires." Paper presented at the American Association for Public Opinion Research meeting, Pheasant Run, Ill., May 1993.

Marín, G., and Marín, B. V. *Research with Hispanic Populations*. Newbury Park, Calif.: Sage, 1991.

Royston, P., Bercini, D., Sirken, M., and Mingay, D. "Questionnaire Design Research Laboratory." *Proceedings of the 1986 American Statistical Association Annual Meeting Section on Survey Research Methods*. Washington, D.C.: American Statistical Association, 1986, 703–707.

Werner, O., and Campbell, D. T. "Translating, Working Through Interpreters and the Problem of Decentering." In R. N. Cohen and R. Cohen (eds.), *A Handbook of Method in Cultural Anthropology*. New York: American Museum of Natural History, 1970.

RUTH B. MCKAY is a behavioral scientist and statistician, U.S. Bureau of Labor Statistics, Washington, D.C.

MARTHA J. BRESLOW is a senior research associate with the Institute for Social Research, Ann Arbor, Michigan.

ROBERTA L. SANGSTER is survey methodologist, Office of Survey Methods Research, U.S. Bureau of Labor Statistics, Washington, D.C.

SUSAN M. GABBARD is a senior associate with Aguirre International, San Mateo, California.

ROBERT W. REYNOLDS is assistant professor of sociology, Weber State University, Ogden, Utah.

JORGE M. NAKAMOTO is a senior associate with Aguirre International, San Mateo, California.

JOHN TARNAI is associate director of the Social and Economic Sciences Research Center, Washington State University, Pullman, Washington.

INDEX

and, 49–50; topic saliency hypothesis, 74. *See also* Household-level factors in nonresponse (survey)

Response effects, survey: acquiescent answers, 30–32, 51–52; consistency effects, 54–55; contrast effects, 54–55; extreme answers, 56–57; no-opinion filter effects, 30, 32; norm of evenhandedness and, 52–54; primacy effects, 57–58; question order effects, 30–31, 52–55, 82; quick answers, 55–56; recency effects, 57–58; social desirability and, 50–51; status quo alternative effects, 30, 32. *See also* Nonresponse, survey

Response rates, survey: decline in, 31; factors affecting, 64–66; factors predicting, 20; maximizing, 20, 63; respondent motivation and, 31; survey translation and, 103; Total Design Method and, 20

Results, survey: additional predictors of, 39–42; cognitive factors and, 33–39, 42; informing the public and, 13–14; interest group politics and, 10–11; interest in, 14; journalists and, 14; mode switching and, 46; respondent educational level and, 42. *See also* Response effects, survey; Satisficing

Rosenthal, R., 34
Ross, M., 23
Rossi, P. H., 4, 5, 8
Royston, P., 95
Rubin, D. B., 63, 77
Rucker, R. E., 73

Sample surveys, 17. *See also* Surveys
Sampling errors, 21. *See also* Error, survey
Sangster, R. L., 53, 55
Satisficing: additional causes of (study), 39–42; cognitive skills and (studies), 33–38; deception and, 42; decision making and, 30; defining, 31–32; educational attainment and, 36, 38, 42; empirical studies of, 33–42; face-to-face interviewing and, 43; future research on, 42; mental coin flipping and, 39; nondifferentiation and, 39; Ohio State University analysis, 36–38; probability formula of, 33; regulators of, 32–33; respondent ability and, 32; respondent cognition need and, 32; respondent motivation and, 32; response strategies of, 31–32; Schuman and Presser's

experiments and, 33–36; Simon's concept of, 30; strong versus weak, 31–32; survey design issues and, 43; task difficulty and, 32

Schaeffer, N. C., 20
Schober, M. F., 83
Schuman, H., 31, 33, 34, 37, 38, 43, 51, 54, 56, 57
Schwarz, N., 22, 24, 47, 51, 53, 54, 55, 58, 59, 82
Schweitzer, J. C., 20
Scott, L. J., 56
Self-administered questionnaires, 17
Sensitive items, 24, 26
Sexual behavior surveys, 24–25
Shadish, W. R., 4
Sheatsley, P. B., 53
Shoemaker, D. M., 90
Sigelman, L., 82
Simon, H. A., 30
Singer, E., 24
Sirken, M., 95
Skinner, S. J., 20
Smith, T. W., 14, 72
Sobell, J., 82
Social and Economics Sciences Research Center (SESRC), 100
Social connectedness hypothesis, 71–73
Social exchange hypotheses, 69–71
Solso, R. L., 57
Status quo alternative effects, 30
Sternberg, R. J., 36
Stokes, L. A., 22
Strack, F., 47, 51, 53, 54
Structured interviews, 17, 29
Sudman, S., 22, 23, 24, 54, 58, 59
Suppes, P., 91
Surveys: civic knowledge and, 5–6; cognitive burden of, 29; cognitive/social psychology and, 29; confidentiality and, 24–25; as data collection tool, 17; evaluation uses of, 4; evaluator role in, 14; general population, 8–9, 14; government policy, 6–7; health care reform and, 6; interest group politics and, 10; journalists and, 14; means-ends use of, 4; mixed-format, 25–26; mode differences and, 45, 50–58; mode switching and, 46; optimizing and, 30, 31; policy makers and, 8–11; political/social, 3; potency of, 3; quality/accuracy of, 4; randomized population, 17; refusal conversion interviewers and, 31; running

ORDERING INFORMATION

NEW DIRECTIONS FOR EVALUATION is a series of paperback books that presents the latest techniques and procedures for conducting useful evaluation studies of all types of programs. Books in the series are published quarterly in Spring, Summer, Fall, and Winter and are available for purchase by subscription as well as by single copy.

SUBSCRIPTIONS for 1996 cost $59.00 for individuals (a savings of 22 percent over single-copy prices) and $87.00 for institutions, agencies, and libraries. Please do not send institutional checks for personal subscriptions. Standing orders are accepted. (For subscriptions outside of North America, add $7.00 for shipping via surface mail or $25.00 for air mail. Orders *must be prepaid* in U.S. dollars by check drawn on a U.S. bank or charged to VISA, MasterCard, or American Express.)

SINGLE COPIES cost $19.00 plus shipping (see below) when payment accompanies order. California, New Jersey, New York, and Washington, D.C., residents please include appropriate sales tax. Canadian residents add GST and any local taxes. Billed orders will be charged shipping and handling. No billed shipments to post office boxes. (Orders from outside North America *must be prepaid* in U.S. dollars by check drawn on a U.S. bank or charged to VISA, MasterCard, or American Express.)

SHIPPING (SINGLE COPIES ONLY): $10.00 and under, add $2.50; to $20.00, add $3.50; to $50.00, add $4.50; to $75.00, add $5.50; to $100.00, add $6.50; to $150.00, add $7.50; over $150.00, add $8.50.

DISCOUNTS FOR QUANTITY ORDERS are available. Please write to the address below for information.

ALL ORDERS must include either the name of an individual or an official purchase order number. Please submit your order as follows:
Subscriptions: specify series and year subscription is to begin
Single copies: include individual title code (such as PE59)

MAIL ALL ORDERS TO:
Jossey-Bass Publishers
350 Sansome Street
San Francisco, California 94104-1342

FOR SUBSCRIPTION SALES OUTSIDE OF THE UNITED STATES, CONTACT:
any international subscription agency or Jossey-Bass directly.

OTHER TITLES AVAILABLE IN THE
NEW DIRECTIONS FOR EVALUATION SERIES
Lois-ellin G. Datta, Editor-in-Chief